PRAISE
CHRISTIAN HIGHER EDUCATION: AN EMPIRICAL GUIDE

"Thanks to Glanzer, Cockle, and Martin for this invaluable book offering readers a new lens for navigating the many approaches to Christian higher education present in the US and Canada today. For those just beginning their Christian higher education journeys, this guide provides an accessible overview of the wide array of institutions with various Christian commitments and expressions. Meanwhile, more experienced scholars and practitioners receive an objective and useable tool for evaluating the way Christian identity influences key institutional practices."

—**Shirley V. Hoogstra**, JD, President,
Council for Christian Colleges & Universities

"*Christian Higher Education: An Empirical Guide* is an indispensable resource that sheds light on the complex and diverse world of Christian colleges and universities. The authors provide a comprehensive analysis, based on empirical measures, to help parents, students, faculty, and staff navigate the overwhelming task of choosing the right institution. With a keen focus on the challenges faced by these groups, the authors address the common concerns of parents investing in their children's education, individuals who have regretted their choices, and disillusioned faculty members or administrators. By exposing the discrepancies between the professed Christian identity and the actual implementation of that identity, the book unveils the varied experiences and missions across campus. This guide equips readers with invaluable knowledge for informed decision-making, ensuring that resources are wisely invested in institutions that align with their values and goals. Whether you are a parent, staff member, faculty, administrators, or board member, *Christian Higher Education* is an eye-opening and essential tool that illuminates the intricate landscape of Christian higher education."

—**Michael J. James**, Director, Institute for Administrators
in Catholic Higher Education Boston College

CHRISTIAN
HIGHER
EDUCATION

.

CHRISTIAN HIGHER EDUCATION

An Empirical Guide

PERRY L. GLANZER, THEODORE F. COCKLE,
AND JESSICA MARTIN

Abilene Christian University Press

CHRISTIAN HIGHER EDUCATION
An Empirical Guide

Contents

INTRODUCTION

Confusion about "Christian" Universities

D uring my (Perry's) academic career researching faith-based higher education in North America and around the world, I have received three types of emails. First, parents often write me with their questions about the confusing array of Christian colleges and universities. They are about to invest hundreds of thousands of dollars, but they realize that unlike buying a house, they have little information by which to evaluate the various types of Christian colleges and universities. They have queries about the differences among Texas Christian University, Southern Methodist University, and Biola University. Two sound more Christian in their names than the other. What are the differences? These parents lack the resources to explain the current landscape and want a guide that can help them.

The second type of email I receive is what I call the "realized too late" email. These parents, students, and sometimes even faculty or staff failed to understand the institutions in which they decided to invest tuition dollars or their lives. For instance, I recently received this email from a Christian faculty member: "After teaching for ten years at [a regional state university], I accepted a post at [an Evangelical Lutheran Church in America (ELCA)] college. I naively assumed that this ELCA college would be deeply rooted in Christian values. What I experienced was deeply disturbing. As a born-again Christian, I experienced more resistance at [this ELCA college] than I did at the 'secular' [regional university]! Following six years at [the ELCA college], I joined the faculty at [a different regional state university]." This faculty member learned a hard truth that other faculty, students, parents, and staff have as well—sometimes too late. Namely, Christian universities are not equal in how they support and embody their Christian identity and missions.

Said another way, it is important to recognize that mentioning a Christian identity in a mission statement does not always influence the decisions of an institution in areas like membership and curricular or cocurricular planning or other administrative decisions in uniform ways. What is more, even when Christian universities *do* put into effect their Christian identity or missions, they do so with such variance that the Christian missions are realized and experienced quite differently on various campuses. Thus, if a parent, student, faculty member, or staff person were to choose a school thinking that Christian identity is somewhat standardized across institutions, they would do so erroneously. They might "realize too late" the tremendous variation that exists across campuses boasting a "Christian campus experience."

The third type of email comes from the discouraged Christian faculty member or administrator. They see their institution prioritizing different aspects of its mission but giving scant attention to the Christian mission or Christian faculty development. They sense that their campus leadership fails to take the Christian identity seriously, but they are having trouble convincing the leadership that some of their decisions have important implications for the Christian identity of the institution. I (Perry) have even written some of those emails or editorials.[1]

This guide is for all three of these groups. In particular, it is for those who care about the Christian college experience but want to learn more about the variety of experiences present on Christian campuses and the specific ways they can make a difference.

UNDERSTANDING THE DIVERSITY OF CHRISTIAN HIGHER EDUCATION

Most people do not realize how unique North American higher education is when compared to the rest of the world. Claims of American exceptionalism can often be exaggerated, but in the case of Christian higher education, the United States truly is exceptional. The Christian diversity present within the US higher education system is the primary basis of its exceptionalism.

This diversity emerged a century after the founding of Harvard by Congregationalists in 1636. Six different religious/secular traditions established eight colleges in the US colonies before the Revolutionary War: William and Mary, founded by Anglicans in 1693; Yale, founded by Congregationalists in 1701; Princeton (originally called the College of New Jersey), founded by Presbyterians in 1746; Columbia, founded by Anglicans in 1754; Penn, started by Quakers but primarily secular, founded in 1755; Brown, founded by Baptists in 1764; Rutgers, founded by the Dutch Reformed in 1766; and Dartmouth, founded by Congregationalists in 1769.[2] Although their entry into higher education in the United States was later than their Protestant counterparts, Catholics founded Georgetown in 1789.

As a result, shortly after its official founding as a nation, the United States contained the most diverse set of religious institutions of higher education in the world. Nowhere else on the globe in 1800 could one find Anglican, Baptist, Catholic, Congregational, Lutheran, Methodist, Presbyterian, and Quaker colleges existing in one country (indeed, the first European Baptist university only originated in the 1990s[3]).

This diversity continued to expand throughout US history. Before the Civil War, fifteen Christian denominations sponsored or helped create 165 of the first 182 colleges in the United States, amounting to over 90 percent of the institutions of higher learning at that time.[4] Today, the United States is home to Christian institutions from sixty-one different Christian traditions and denominations. There is also significant diversity within some of the larger traditions. For example, institutions affiliated with the Catholic Church are often sponsored by one of several orders—each bringing unique emphases to their approaches to higher education. Thus, to understand the differences among Christian institutions, one needs to understand the differences among Christian traditions and denominations.

Of course, Christian universities do not always stay Christian. When Christian universities discard the distinctions that make them Christian, the process is called secularization. Secularization, broadly defined, is the process of disassociation from a faith tradition—often to maintain the classically liberal neutrality required of a democracy. Rather than the result of a single decision, secularization is generally considered to be the result of several small decisions that subtly shift an entity away from its religious moorings over time. C. John Sommerville helpfully notes that there are five types of secularization discussed by scholars.[5] When discussing secularization, scholars may refer to the secularization of society, institutions, activities, populations, mentalities, or some combination of these five. In this book, we are primarily interested in *institutional* secularization. In other words, we will not be examining whether faculty or students pray less, believe in God less, or hold fewer voluntary Bible studies. The focus of this work is on the secularization that happens at an institutional level as a result of the administrative actions of universities as found in administrative policies.

As many people know, most of the biggest names in US higher education were founded by Protestant denominations but have since been completely secularized. These include the highest-ranking institutions of higher education in the United States: Harvard, Yale, Princeton, Columbia, University of Chicago, Duke, Northwestern, Dartmouth, Brown, Vanderbilt, Emory, and many more.[6] Interestingly, although a few Catholic institutions have secularized, such as Weber, College of Santa Fe, and Dominican, almost all their elite institutions, such as the University of Notre Dame, Boston College, and Villanova, are still robustly Catholic (see Chapter Four for a broader discussion). But what about the rest of the colleges and universities with historic ties to

Christianity? Or what about colleges that still claim Christianity—what are the different ways they embody their Christian missions? If you are wondering which contemporary institutions currently use their Christian identity in institutional decision-making, then keep reading. One of the primary goals of our book is to help you understand the various degrees to which institutions operationalize their Christian identity.

OVERVIEW, AUDIENCE, AND DEFINITIONS

So how can future administrators, faculty, and staff understand the various types of Christian higher education, the degree to which they have perhaps secularized, and the different elements of a university? After all, there are hundreds of Christian colleges and universities in the United States and Canada as well as thousands around the world. The purpose of this book is to provide readers with a guide through the field of Christian higher education in the United States and Canada.

To facilitate this tour, we created the Operationalizing Christian Identity Guide (OCIG) to identify the major ways that Christian colleges and universities use their Christian identity to make mission, marketing, membership, curricular, cocurricular, and other administrative decisions. The OCIG is composed of markers that can be identified by anyone, no matter their religious or nonreligious background. This book relies on our empirical guide to tour through Protestant, Catholic, and Eastern Orthodox institutions in the United States and Canada.

Before starting this tour, it will be helpful to define some key terms. First, we need to address the following: What is a college or university? In English-speaking North America, these terms are often used interchangeably, but we want to be clear on what we mean when we use such terms. In this volume, we are primarily interested in distinguishing *multidisciplinary* colleges and universities from other institutions. We define such a college or university as an institution that is a baccalaureate college, master's college, and university or doctoral-granting institution. We do not include special-focus institutions such as seminaries, teachers colleges, schools of engineering and technology, or associate's colleges.

We also do not include Bible colleges, which do not offer majors in at least two distinct areas of study beyond Christianity or church vocations.

The second important definitional issue that needs to be addressed is what counts as "Christian." We will define Christian institutions in this book as those associated with the three main branches of the Christian Church: the Eastern Orthodox, Protestant, and Roman Catholic traditions. What makes such a college or university Christian? The answer to that question is the subject of the first chapter.

CHAPTER 1

What Makes a University Christian?

The major problem we face as we seek to describe what makes a university Christian is that there exists no clear way of evaluating the centrality of institutional faith commitments in the vast field of Christian higher education. Current approaches require extensive knowledge of the system to begin to see differences. This chapter addresses this problem by setting forth a clear way to assess the Christian higher education landscape while providing insight into its important features. Before we describe our method, however, we want to set forth the current problem in more detail.

THE LIMITS OF EARLIER APPROACHES

Early US higher education leaders rarely used the term *Christian* to distinguish their institutions. Most of higher education was understood to be Christian at the time—even those colleges that received colonial funding and, after the Revolutionary War, state funding. If there was a common adjective used to describe what we now call private Christian colleges, it was *sectarian* or *denominational*, since Christian colleges were understood through the lens of Protestant denominational affiliation.

A different set of terms, however, began to be used in the 1930s that drew upon the word *church* to describe these institutions. These included *church-sponsored*, *church-affiliated*, and most often, *church-related*. The latter, more dominant term—*church-related*—gained prevalence with the formation of the National Council of Church-Related Colleges in 1932.[1]

What was the reason for the emerging popularity of this term? One scholar astutely observes, "The growing usage of this phrase reflected the growing sense of *distance* between church and college."[2] The distance pertained to the decreasing role of the churches in funding higher education, the rise of a US legal tradition that increasingly limited state sponsorship of denominational education, and the reticence of groups such as the Carnegie Foundation to fund sectarian (denominationally exclusive) institutions.[3]

The growing distance between church and college created a noticeable tension for institutions with ties to a church or denomination. Their willingness to identify as "church-related" depended on who was doing the asking: "If it was the denomination that was doing the asking, then the college's answer was likely to be 'Yes' . . . if it was the general public, the Federal Government, or some secular agency that was doing the asking, then the college's answer may well have been negative."[4] In other words, the introduction of the Establishment Clause of the First Amendment in 1791, which later became applied to the states as well in the twentieth century, meant that state governments began to oppose the funding of sectarian, denominational, or church-related colleges.

Given this intentional distancing of some colleges from their sponsoring denominations, Richard G. Hutcheson raised this question in 1988: "Are church-related colleges also Christian colleges?" His answer was "not necessarily," and he identified markers that he believed characterized a church-related, Christian college, which he described as "an institution that would directly, forthrightly and publicly acknowledge its Christian dimension."[5]

Not everyone agreed with Hutcheson's approach. Merrimon Cuningim, a defender of the High Church Protestant "church-related" label, claimed that the term *Christian*, with reference to higher education, was "apt to be a battle cry, or seem so to the whitewashed inside or the unwashed outside."[6] Unfortunately, Cuninggim failed to acknowledge that the use of "church-related" resulted in the inability to make simple distinctions between an institution such as Biola University, which is not church-related but uses its Christian identity to guide administrative decision-making in multiple areas, and Texas Christian University (TCU) or Duke University, which have no empirical markers of a Christian identity but are sometimes still referred to as church-related. Under Cuninggim's approach, there is no battle cry, but there is also no helpful language for distinguishing among institutions with obvious differences.

To be more specific, recent vocabulary for Christian institutions presents three problems. First, consider the most popular recent term, *church-related*. One can be "related" to another person, institution, or idea to varying degrees. For example, a big difference exists between being a sibling and being a fourth cousin. Just as we have a wide variety of family relationships, Christian institutions have a wide variety of relationships with their Christian identity. The Christian identity of some institutions guides essential decisions about membership, curriculum, and policy, whereas other institutions function much like secular state institutions, their Christian identity influencing relatively few decisions.

Second, the emphasis on denominational or church affiliation terminology ignores and downplays the existence of one of the unique creations of the United States—the non-, multi-, or interdenominational Christian college or university.[7] Contemporary institutions like Biola University and Wheaton College (Illinois) are neither officially "denominational" nor "church-related" in any traditional sense. Still, their Christian identity thoroughly influences their missions, curricula, and outcomes.

Third and most importantly, the term confuses parents, faculty, and even the public. Far too often, mass media depicts college-going in the United States as a monolithic experience, but that could not be further from the truth. Differences in the structures, approaches, and missions of schools lead to entirely different success outcomes. Thus, it behooves those who study higher education to make clear distinctions among different types of schools as an act of honesty to both the student and the institution itself.

Those looking for other ways to learn about a Christian institution could simply turn to random internet rankings. For example, we found one such ranking on EdSmart.[8] This site ranks Christian colleges based on cost, graduation rate, retention rate, and the median earnings of graduates ten years after attending the school. Although these metrics are helpful, it is interesting that one would rank the best Christian college based on two financial factors and two factors that—though identical to the metrics by which secular universities are measured—reveal nothing about the seriousness with which the institution takes its Christian mission (or if it even has a Christian mission).

Unfortunately, asking colleges that are in the business of recruiting students about these distinctions is no better. Admissions officers and tour guides are generally taught to downplay controversy and market the university. It is reasonable for schools to market themselves in the best possible light, but parents and students, future faculty and staff, and the public need resources that move beyond marketing rhetoric to see what the Christian commitment of a school means in practice.

Consequently, the terminology we use in speaking about Christian institutions must be unhampered by broad, outdated categories. To accomplish this end, we need clear and objective institutional markers that are agreeable to a wide range of higher education scholars regardless of religious or nonreligious identity. In this book, we set forth a method of evaluating the influence a Christian identity has on an institution using eleven clear markers related to its mission, rhetoric, membership requirements, curriculum, cocurriculum, and governance. We then apply the resultant Operationalizing Christian Identity Guide (OCIG) to evaluate institutions. By "operationalize," we mean that the specific markers we assess serve as evidence of *how various Christian universities put their Christian identity into effect through concrete (i.e., observable) actions or policies.* Overall, we believe the OCIG provides the clearest understanding of the diverse ways that institutions demonstrate their relationship to a Christian identity to date.

THE OPERATIONALIZING CHRISTIAN
IDENTITY GUIDE (OCIG)

Every institution has certain publicly expressed markers that indicate if and how the Christian identity made a difference in key administrative decisions regarding the life of the institution. Any person, no matter what their religious beliefs, can identify these markers. Thus, a numbering system that identifies and adds up these markers can provide a better appraisal of the weight an institution gives its faith-based identity within administrative, curricular, and cocurricular decisions. Rather than distinct categories that may misrepresent areas of faith-based emphasis, the OCIG places Christian institutions along a continuum.

Based on our review of the scholarship of Christian higher education and the research of our team, we selected eleven administrative decisions that—together—give an empirical picture of the influence of an institution's faith-based identity on practice. In addition to their importance, we also selected these eleven decisions based on their ability to be classified with clearly defined criteria. Thus, these decisions—which form the basis for the OCIG—reveal significant areas where faith has informed practice. These markers do not and cannot capture every possible manifestation of the Christian mission on a given campus. For example, our guide does not measure the extent to which a professor integrates faith into a given class. That said, we believe these indicators provide a basic—albeit important—empirical baseline to guide our audience through the various ways the Christian identity influences many administrative decisions. In the coming pages, we will briefly outline the eleven decisions and the criteria we used to rate the approach of an institution.

Mission

The mission statement of a university is the first place to look to find out if it even identifies itself as Christian. TCU explains that its mission is "to educate individuals to think and act as ethical leaders and responsible citizens in a global community."[9] In contrast, the mission of Biola University "is biblically centered education, scholarship, and service—equipping men and women in mind and character to impact the world for the Lord Jesus Christ."[10] For secularized institutions, Jesus and God are absent from the mission. Instead, they usually speak in ethical or educational language while avoiding theological language. The research team used the following codes to classify the mission statements. The point numbers we assigned to each administrative decision are indicated in parentheses:

- Protestant denominational or Catholic order identity, as well as Christian identity, affirmed (2)

- Mission statement says they are "affiliated" with a certain denomination but does not provide any additional signifying Christian language or identity as Christian (1)

- Acknowledges *historical* connection (0)

- Neither Christian nor denominational identity language exists in the mission statement (0)

First-Page Rhetoric

We also looked at the first page of the website to see how an institution identified itself. Specifically, we looked for any theologically informed identity language that indicated the institution was Christian (e.g., "Christian," "Christ-centered"). To be clear, explicitly Christian language moves beyond the simple moral language (e.g., "Come learn how to serve") that one might find at a secular institution. We used the following codes:

- EC: Explicitly Christian (1)

- NC: No distinctively Christian language (0)

"About Us" Rhetoric

Looking at the "About Us" page, which is usually a bit more hidden, offers additional insight into how the institution publicly presents its identity as explicitly Christian or denominational or seems to mask this identity by using no distinctively Christian language. We used the following coding system:

- Explicitly Christian or explicitly denominational (1)

- No distinctively Christian language (0)

Membership Requirements

We wanted to find out who can join and lead the community. Are the students, staff, faculty, president, and/or members of the governance board required to be Christian (e.g., Biola or Taylor University or Wheaton College)? Is it some kind of mixture (such as at Baylor University or the University of Notre Dame)? Or are there no religious requirements for anyone (e.g., Wake Forest University)? Thus, we looked at student admissions pages or applications along with faculty/staff hiring pages to understand if the institution requires students, faculty, and staff to sign statements of faith or affirm a Christian identity. We then used the following coding system:

- Christian identity requirements for students (1)

- Christian identity or belief requirements for faculty (1 for all or 0.5 if part)

- Christian identity or belief requirements for staff (1)

- Christian identity or membership requirements for the president (1)

- Christian/church/denominational/order requirements for being on the governance board (1 for all or 0.5 if part)

- No identity requirements (0)

Vice President for Mission or Chaplain in the President's Executive Cabinet or Leadership Team

This criterion helps you determine if someone on the president's executive team is specifically tasked with making sure the decisions being made consider the Christian mission. Although these positions may exist at an institution and not be on the executive cabinet, we think it is significant whether this person has a voice on the executive committee. We used the following codes:

- Yes (1)

- No (0)

Specific Christian Academic Department

This category refers to the name of the department of the institution that deals with religion, Christianity, the Bible, and so on. This criterion indicates an administrative decision to devote a department to the study of Christianity (e.g., theology, biblical studies, or Christian studies) versus religious studies (which includes the study of non-Christian traditions and mirrors what would occur in a secular university). To put it another way, secular or secularized institutions do not have theology departments. They have religious studies or religion departments. We used the following codes:

- Specific Christian academic department (1)

- Absent or only refers to religion (0)

Required Christian Bible/Theology Classes

Seventh, we wanted to find out if there are any required courses related to Christianity. To start, we looked in the student handbook or academic catalog for the number of required courses in this area. Requiring just one or two general religion courses with plenty of non-Christian options from which students can choose indicates the institution is likely not that serious about passing along the Christian tradition (e.g., most every Methodist, Presbyterian USA, or United Church of Christ institution). If students are required to take thirty hours (ten classes) and receive a minor in Bible (e.g., Biola University) or biblical studies, there is good reason to believe the institution takes educating students in the Christian tradition seriously. We scored up to ten required courses on a scale from zero to ten.

Explicitly Christian Centers or Institutes

This requirement tells you whether there is a particular research focus on Christian topics at the institution. For example, Wheaton College (IL) has the Center for Faith and Innovation, which exists "to develop Christian marketplace leaders through theology and liberal arts research to create innovative solutions for business." We were looking for distinctly Christian approaches; thus we did not include centers addressing general religious or moral questions that one would also find at a secular university (e.g., a bioethics center). We used the following codes:

- One or more (1)

- None (0)

Chapel/Mass

This section evaluates the presence and nature of chapel or mass on a given campus. We gave the required chapel additional weight because it reveals an additional prioritization given to Christian worship on campus over and above merely offering chapel. However, we recognized voluntary Christian chapel that is privileged (i.e., the university gives it a special time, place, and building and does not do the same for other religious traditions given) is distinct from merely having voluntary Christian worship as one option among many religious offerings. Of course, some campuses offer no chapel or mass at all. We captured these distinctions with the following codes:

- Required chapel/mass (2)

- Voluntary university chapel/mass privileged (1)

- Multifaith (0)

- No university chapel/mass (0)

Only Christian Student Groups

The decision to charter an official student religious group reveals a lot about what the leadership of a school deems normal or acceptable on their campus. Campuses with only Christian groups are recognized for clear commitments to retaining a distinctly Christian identity. If schools charter groups for Jewish, Muslim, or Hindu students, they signal that such students exist in their student body, and they are devoting funds to ensure their development in their respective faiths. Of course, it is impossible to tell if having only Christian student groups is the result of an intentional administrative decision or simply a lack of religious diversity in the student body. Though we acknowledge this limitation, the existence of official non-Christian student groups reveals something about the campus ethos. Campuses willing to sponsor student groups representing various religions follow the model of US public pluralism. This led us to code according to the following categories:

- C: Only Christian student groups exist on campus (1)

- MF: Non-Christian religious groups exist on campus (0)

- NRG: No student religious groups on the campus (0)

Code of Conduct Reasoning

We examined the aspirational student life ethos, especially as it is defined through student handbooks. Here, we note there are four types of Christian institutions. Some seek to enforce the law in residence life and focus much of the formation on making sure the liberal democratic virtue of autonomy is respected (e.g., get sexual consent, don't drink and drive). These schools also have current legal definitions regarding race, gender, sexuality, and so on. Then, there are other Christian institutions that seek to enforce an alternative moral standard, perhaps using an honor code, but offer no Christian reasoning for the ethical parts of the code to students. Usually, such codes consist of lists of general virtues you would find at any higher learning institution, such as "respect," "responsibility," "honesty," "kindness," and so on. Students are simply socialized by university authorities into behaving within broadly accepted norms of virtue.

There are also Christian institutions that stipulate ethical guidelines (e.g., no sex outside of marriage, no alcohol) but focus solely on the rules without providing a positive Christian vision of sex, alcohol, and community life. Finally, some institutions offer a community covenant (often complete with biblical or Christian rationales for the different parts of the covenant) that sets forth a positive Christian vision for students about community, stewardship, sexuality, and so on. They ask students to sign these covenants and abide by them. These institutions have put tremendous thought into how their community will seek to live out a Christian educational life together, grounded in mutual accountability (versus taking a simple top-down approach like rule-focused institutions). We located the code of conduct, community covenant, or other student handbook conduct documents and classified them as follows:

- CC: Christian covenant (2). The institution has a separate community covenant or pledge that is made to God and the community and is theologically based.

- CR: Christian reasoning (2). The student handbook refers to explicitly Christian language and reasoning to justify community standards or codes (e.g., sexual conduct).

- CM: Christianity mentioned (1). The document mentions something related to Christianity, perhaps in the preface, although the rest of it consists of independent moral principles/virtues.

- M: Moral (0). The conduct document appeals to broad moral language to substantiate standards.

- L: Legal (0). The student handbook code does not use explicitly Christian language. Instead, it reads much more like a legal document found at pluralistic institutions.

POINT TOTALS AND WHAT THEY
MEAN (AND DON'T MEAN)

The total possible number of points for a single institution is twenty-seven. To be clear, the OCIG neither measures the influences of various decisions nor implies that all decisions are equivalent. For example, the influence of having a vice president for mission or required religion courses may be more or less important than other factors in the Christian mission. Therefore, we note the OCIG simply quantifies the number of *instances* an institution has made administrative, curricular, and cocurricular decisions that distinguish it from a state or private secular university based on its Christian identity. Our guide also seeks to differentiate among different types of decisions Christian institutions make to help guide those interested in navigating the diversity of Christian higher education.

We must make a few additional qualifications. First, the OCIG also does not attempt to measure the religious beliefs, belonging, or behavior of the university community members. In the future, that data could be used to provide such an extension of this scale. Second, this scale only scores administrative decisions on their face. It does not (and cannot) reveal whether the decisions were made for theological or Christian reasons. For instance, an institution with no membership requirements—for which we score 0—may rationalize this decision based on wanting to be hospitable to all different types of students, faculty, administrators, and so on, since the Bible teaches hospitality to the stranger. The former is judged, while the latter is hidden. In other words, this scale *alone* should not necessarily be considered a measure of how Christian or committed to the faith an institution is. Rather, it is a measure of whether faith identity shapes particular administrative choices in ways that are distinct from those found at secular universities. It is meant to provide a baseline for further evaluation by highlighting areas of nuance among various Christian colleges and universities. We do claim, however, that if an institution does not make any choices according to its faith identity, it should not be classified as a faith-based institution.

Finally, we want to be clear that the presence of these factors alone does not make an institution robustly Christian. Although the administrative structures our guide reveals do help or hinder a Christian culture, ultimately, people make the most difference. A student could be required to take four courses about Christianity, but if taught by horrible professors who bore them to tears, they might wonder why they did not attend State Party U with the rest of their friends. Similarly, a person might attend an institution with a theologically rich community covenant ruled by an authoritative resident assistant who has no understanding of how to develop the character or spiritual lives of students. Our guide only measures institutional decision-making, and it cannot be used to evaluate the nature of the Christian culture of an institution.

HOW MANY CHRISTIAN COLLEGES AND UNIVERSITIES EXIST?

Given the difficulties of language and the range of ways of enacting a Christian mission, you may be wondering how many Christian colleges and universities exist. On the internet, you will find a wide range of numbers listed for religious colleges and universities (e.g., 980, 900).[11] The most reliable source, however, places the number at 866 religious postsecondary institutions.[12] Yet this number includes Bible colleges, seminaries, and other institutions that do not fit the definition of an undergraduate multidisciplinary Christian college or university used in this volume. When we undertook our analysis using our definition and lists from scholarly sources, our initial master list of institutions included only 665 colleges and universities. This list shrank even more when applying our framework. Some others who responded and stated that they are not religious were removed, and still, others who had zero points were removed. Plus, we should note that this list is constantly in flux. For example, even in the relatively short time it took us to revise the manuscript through the publication process, we learned that three different institutions on our list were closing, one was reverting back to being a Bible college, and one new institution had been created. In the end, our team identified 546 Christian colleges and universities in the United States (366 Protestant, 179 Catholic, and 1 Eastern Orthodox) and 16 institutions in Canada (5 Catholic and 11 Protestant). We should note that all of our institutional analysis is based on our findings through April 2023. The following chapters provide some insight into the diversity of these institutions.

CHAPTER 2

Mainline Protestant Colleges and Universities

The first Christian institutions that originated in the United States—including schools like Harvard (1636), Yale (1701), and Princeton (1746)—were started by Protestant Christian denominations usually labeled as mainline Protestant.[1] The major denominations commonly classified as mainline Protestant today are the following:

- American Baptist Churches
- Christian Church (Disciples of Christ)
- Church of the Brethren
- Congregationalist
- Episcopal Church
- Evangelical Lutheran Church in America (ELCA)
- United Methodist Church
- Moravian Church in North America
- Presbyterian Church (USA)
- Reformed Church in America
- Religious Society of Friends (Quakers)
- United Church of Christ

These dominations played a vital role in starting over three-fourths of all US colleges before the Civil War (the rest being either state or Roman Catholic institutions; see Table 2.1).

Table 2.1. Mainline Protestant Colleges Started before the Civil War

Denomination	Number
Presbyterian	49
Methodist	34
Baptist	25
Congregational	21
Anglican/Episcopal	11
Lutheran	6
Disciples of Christ	5
German Reformed	4
Quakers/Friends	2
Christian	1
Dutch Reformed	1
United Brethren	1

Note: N = 160.

Source: Donald G. Tewksbury, *The Founding of American Colleges and Universities before the Civil War* (New York: Teacher College Press, 1932), 32–54.

The degree to which the Christian identity influenced these early colleges varied depending on the institution. When it came to Christian identity and practice, the presidents expected the professors to be Christian, students to attend chapel, and both to follow Christian moral standards. Yet the required classical curriculum was often short on Christian scriptures and theology. Students were primarily expected to pick up their knowledge of the Bible and theology in the chapel and were only required to take a moral philosophy capstone course, which by the late nineteenth century was increasingly secularized and eventually disbanded. Still, Christianity influenced significant parts of Christian colleges and universities before the US Civil War.[2]

Although the three schools mentioned previously (and many other mainline institutions) have fully secularized, a number of mainline colleges and universities still demonstrate some Christian elements. This chapter will cover institutions associated with mainline denominations that still show some sign of a Christian identity. A few of these colleges (a couple of American Baptist and Quaker institutions) are part of the Council for Christian Colleges and Universities (CCCU) and will therefore be included in the discussion of CCCU institutions in Chapter Five.

MANY MAINLINE PROTESTANT INSTITUTIONS HAVE SECULARIZED

As mentioned in the Introduction, one of the problems with identifying Protestant institutions of higher education today is determining the degree to which they have secularized. Applying the Operationalizing Christian Identity Guide (OCIG) outlined in Chapter One helps resolve that issue. For instance, utilizing the OCIG, we identified 49 surviving mainline Protestant institutions among the 160 that started before the Civil War. Additionally, there are 71 that fit this category that started during or after the Civil War (1861 or after).

In total, we found 120 mainline Protestant institutions of higher education that still exhibit some remnant of a Christian identity. Thus, despite having "Christian" or a denomination in their names and mentioning their Christian heritage, institutions like Texas Christian University and Southern Methodist University (SMU) were found to be secular universities by our identifiable empirical standards.

Almost all these completely secularized institutions are associated with the American Baptist Churches, the Disciples of Christ, the ELCA, the Presbyterian Church (USA), the United Church of Christ, and the United Methodist Church. Although denominations may still claim some sort of church relationship to institutions such as Duke, Emory, SMU, and so on, these institutions do not demonstrate any sign of a Christian identity beyond names and historical association.[3]

LARGELY SECULARIZED WITH MINIMAL CHRISTIAN INFLUENCE (1 TO 5.5)

Of the 120 mainline institutions with some remnant of a Christian identity, 89 of them, almost three-quarters, operationalize it in minimal ways (scoring between 1 and 5.5). In general, there are two areas where these institutions still operationalize some influence: a mention of Christian affiliation in the mission and allowing favoritism toward Christian worship on campus (see Table 2.2).

Table 2.2. Key Distinctives of Largely Secularized Mainline Institutions

Operationalized Distinctive	% of Institutions with Distinctive
Privilege Christian Worship	75
Christian Affiliation Affirmed in the Mission	58

Note: N = 89.

For most of these institutions, the affirmation of Christian affiliation is tucked away from view; only three of them mention their Christian or denominational identity on the home pages of their websites. Furthermore, only 15 percent require students to take a course that focuses on the Christian tradition. In other words, 85 percent have no curricular requirement that seeks to establish any form of basic Christian literacy or theological thinking among students.

SOME CHRISTIAN INFLUENCE (6 TO 8.5)

The remaining 26 percent of mainline institutions exhibit more significant Christian influence and can be divided into two broad categories. The first set, which scores from 6 to 8.5 on the OCIG, is largely ELCA institutions (46 percent), with a sprinkling of other denominations (see Table 2.3).

Table 2.3. OCIG Scores of Mainline Institutions with Some Surviving Christian Influence

Institution Name	Denomination	OCIG Score
Augustana University (SD)	ELCA	6
Emory and Henry College	United Methodist	6
Ottawa University	American Baptist	6
Westminster College (PA)	Presbyterian USA	6
Concordia College (Morehead, MN)	ELCA	6.5
Texas Lutheran College	ELCA	6.5
Tusculum University	Presbyterian USA	6.5
William Penn University	Quakers	6.5
Alderson Broaddus University	American Baptist	7
Amridge University (AL)	United Church of Christ	7
Augsburg College	ELCA	7
California Lutheran University	ELCA	7
Newberry College	ELCA	7
Ashland University	Brethren	7.5
Gustavus Adolphus College	ELCA	7.5
Wilmington College	Quakers	7.5
Bethany College (WV)	ELCA	8
McMurry University	United Methodist	8
University of Jamestown	Presbyterian USA	8
Bethel University (TN)	Cumberland Presbyterian	8.5
Luther College	ELCA	8.5
Valparaiso University	ELCA	8.5

What makes these institutions different from the largely secularized mainline colleges and universities is that 64 percent affirm a Christian mission (versus stating an affiliation), and 68 percent are willing to require students to take one course about the Christian tradition (see Table 2.4). Furthermore, close to half (46 percent) require the president to be Christian.

Table 2.4. Key Distinctives of Mainline Institutions with Some Surviving Christian Influence

Operationalized Distinctive	%
Privilege Christian Worship	86
Require a Christian Course	68
Christian Mission (versus Affiliation)	64
"About Us" Page Mentions Christian Identity	59
Require Church Membership or Christian Identity for President	46
VP for Mission / Chaplain on Executive Leadership Team	36
Christian Reasoning in Student Conduct Code	36
First Web Page Mentions Christian Identity	32
Christian Department	18
Require Christian Membership for Students, Staff, or Faculty	0

Note: N = 22.

Still, only 18 percent have an academic department devoted to Christianity, only 32 percent affirm a Christian identity on the first web page, and not one of them requires all their staff or faculty to be Christian.

SIGNIFICANT CHRISTIAN INFLUENCE (10+)

There are only nine mainline Protestant institutions unaffiliated with the CCCU that operationalize their Christian identity in ways that significantly influence their functions (scoring over 10; see Table 2.5).

Table 2.5. OCIG Scores of Mainline Institutions with Persevering Christian Influence

Institution Name	Denomination	OCIG Score
Huntingdon College	United Methodist	11
University of Dubuque	Presbyterian USA	11
Hope College	Reformed Church in America	11.5
Waynesburg University	Presbyterian USA	12
Concordia University (St. Paul, MN)	Lutheran–Missouri Synod	13
Concordia University (TX)	Lutheran–Missouri Synod	13
Barclay College	Quakers	14
University of Sioux Falls	American Baptist	14
Oklahoma Wesleyan University	Wesleyan Methodist Church	18

Bolstering the scores of these institutions is the fact that 100 percent privilege Christian worship, identify as Christian on their "About Us" page, and require a Christian course, and 33 percent even require chapel (see Table 2.6). Furthermore, 89 percent affirm a Christian mission, and 67 percent mention their Christian identity on the home page. Additionally, 67 percent have a Christian department, require two Christian courses, and use Christian moral reasoning in their student conduct codes. Not surprisingly, 89 percent have requirements that the president be Christian, 67 percent have requirements that faculty be Christian, and 56 percent have similar staff requirements.

Table 2.6. Key Distinctives of Mainline Institutions with Persevering Christian Influence

Operationalized Distinctive	%
Privilege Christian Worship	100
"About Us" Page Mentions Christian Identity	100
Require Christian Courses (1+)	100
Christian Mission (versus Affiliation)	89
Require Church Membership or Christian Identity for President	89
Christian Department	67
First Web Page Mentions Christian Identity	67
Require Christian Courses (2+)	67
Christian Reasoning in Student Conduct Code	67
Require Faculty to Be Christian	67
Require Staff to Be Christian	56
Require Christian Chapel	33
Require Christian Courses (3+)	22
Require Students to Be Christian	0

Note: N = 9.

For those wanting to attend or work at a mainline Protestant institution that operationalizes its commitment to a Christian identity and mission in clear ways, these nine institutions represent choices consistent with that desire. Interestingly, these institutions are virtually all located in the central part of the United States.

CONCLUSION

The empirical reality is that most mainline Protestant universities and colleges do not operationalize their Christian identity to any significant degree—93 percent score less than 10 on the OCIG. Furthermore, there does not appear to be any interest among mainline Protestant denominations in starting new institutions. They have not started any new institutions in close to half a century and have only started fifteen in the past one hundred years. In addition, many of the remaining institutions that presently exist are small.

The state of mainline Protestant institutions is best represented by one particular finding. A little over two decades ago, both St. Olaf and Valparaiso were praised by Robert Benne, one of the scholars who influenced our development of the OCIG, for demonstrating what he called "quality with soul."[4] Now, Valparaiso scores 8.5, and St. Olaf only scores 5.5. In other words, St. Olaf now only minimally operationalizes its Christian identity. Although there are nine outliers among mainline Protestant institutions, one must look beyond mainline Protestantism to discover the bulk of institutions that operationalize their Christian identity in significant ways.

CHAPTER 3

Historically Black Colleges and Universities (HBCUs)

After the Civil War, the four million newly freed Black people in the United States faced an uncertain, turbulent future. They were largely disenfranchised, lacking consistent legal protection. Into this void, Christian missionary associations offered their help. Institutions such as the American Baptist Home Mission Society, the American Missionary Association (AMA) of the Congregational Church, the Freedmen's Aid Society of the Methodist Episcopal Church, and the Board of Missions for Freedmen of the Presbyterian Church supported education and the well-being of many. Then, in 1865, the Freedmen's Bureau funded mass education, creating K-12 schools and the first historically Black colleges and universities (HBCUs), such as Fisk University (1866), Howard University (1867), and Augusta Institute (later Morehouse College; 1868).

Of these groups, the AMA provides a fascinating and inspiring case study. It was originally formed in 1846 to provide support for the kidnapped Africans from the Amistad (the story on which the well-known movie *The Amistad* is based). Henry Drewry and Humphrey Doermann note in their history of private HBCUs, "This organization became one of the most productive religious groups working to establish black schools and colleges. As late as 1915, it supported thirty institutions serving seven thousand students in eleven southern states."[1]

The AMA and other Northern supporting agencies persevered in their work, even after the Freedmen's Bureau was discontinued by Congress in 1872. Though often lacking in funds, they viewed their philanthropy as God ordained, and they made certain that their sponsoring institutions knew how much they had given on their behalf. This 1876 description by the founders of the Fisk University of today shows how the leaders of the school could rehearse what they had been told: "The emancipation of the slaves by the war . . . stirred most profoundly the hearts of Northern people. It was felt that only by education and religious culture could they be fitted for their new sphere—that to this end they needed help and needed it immediately. . . . Nearly all denominations of Christians in the Northern States were aroused to activity and sent missionaries and teachers to follow up the march of the army; so that schools quickly took the place of encampments."[2]

Without question, many HBCUs that are thriving today owe their origins to Northern Christian philanthropy. Yet a romanticized account, such as the one provided previously, paints an incomplete picture. James D. Anderson's critical historical account titled *The Education of Blacks in the South, 1860–1935* provides a more complete telling of the complex political, cultural, and social motivations and implications of Northern and Southern financial support for HBCUs. The following summary of his book-length account provides a helpful supplement to the Fisk founders' statement of indebtedness: "Initially, ex-slaves attempted to create an educational system that would support and extend their emancipation, but their children were pushed into a system of industrial education that presupposed Black political and economic subordination. . . . Because Blacks lacked economic and political power, White elites were able to control the structure and content of black education during the first third of the twentieth century. Nonetheless, Blacks persisted in their struggle to develop an educational system in accordance with their own needs and desires."[3] As part of these efforts, recently constituted African American Christian denominations formed their own institutions or took over earlier ones. For example, the African Methodist Episcopal (AME) Church took over Wilberforce University (1863) and started Allen College (1870). Similarly, the African American Episcopal Zion denomination formed Livingston College (1879). These institutions were particularly important for developing Black leadership. For instance, Cynthia L. Jackson and Eleanor F. Nunn note, "Except for HBCUs affiliated with Black church organizations, the majority of the early presidents of HBCUs were White."[4] Although they severely lacked funds, such African American denominations viewed their work as God ordained; they also viewed the finances that allowed them to persevere as providential.[5]

THE EARLY CHRISTIAN INFLUENCE

Considering this history, it is not surprising that the Christian tradition significantly shaped the mission, administration, curriculum, and cocurriculum of these early institutions. The centrality of the Christian mission can be found in early mottos. Fisk's motto was "the development of Christian manhood in an education for service."[6] Spelman College, one of the early female colleges founded in a Baptist church in 1881, chose as its motto "Our Whole School for Christ,"[7] and the early 1904 catalog of Tougaloo College summarized the intent for the whole institution to be "lit by morality and transfused with the religion of the Christ, to the end that it may attain the highest of goals."[8] As these examples demonstrate, early HBCUs prioritized Christian rhetoric.

Policies related to membership imitated the early White mainline Protestant universities. Administrators and faculty of all these early institutions were Christian, and most of the early presidents were ministers. Indeed, the financial resources from the North were often entrusted to emerging Black Christian leaders of these institutions. Some of these important Christian leaders included Mordecai Johnson (first African American president of Howard University), Benjamin E. Mays (president of Morehouse College), Bishop Daniel Payne with the African American Methodist Episcopal Church (founder of Wilberforce University), Baptist

Richard C. Coulter (cofounder of Morehouse), and Baptist Rev. Edmund Turney (cofounder of Morehouse).[9] The church sometimes provided even more than leadership. For instance, Morehouse was founded in a Baptist church.

The Christian emphasis in the curriculum often followed the classical curriculum of White institutions of the time. Thus, required courses had less to do with biblical and/or theological study, which was expected to be transmitted through church and chapel. Instead, the classical curriculum often required more pagan Greek and Roman authors than Christian scriptures and theology. The major exception was that of Christian moral formation, as the early curriculum of HBCUs included the same capstone moral philosophy course common at White mainline Protestant institutions.

As such, the bulk of the faith and moral formation occurred through the cocurricular dimension of the universities. It is not clear from available institutional histories if students were required to be Christian, but they were required to attend church and chapel, regulate their relationship between the sexes, avoid drinking and playing billiards, and—if the school was Baptist—avoid dancing. At Fisk, students were required to attend Sunday church service and Sunday school, as well as daily chapels. Men, however, could not escort women to these events. Dating was also strictly regulated such that "if a young man dated a young lady twice, he had to call on another girl before escorting the former again."[10]

Some went even further. As Drewry and Doermann note, "Women could not receive male callers at Tougaloo College; the matrons at Storer College maintained the right to inspect incoming mail; and rules at Lane College stipulated what students were to wear right down to their undergarments!"[11] Later in the 1900s, after student rebellions, some rules changed (e.g., prohibitions against smoking or playing billiards), and the focus shifted to providing students with a robust student organizational life like that found at White institutions. For example, Howard University strongly promoted the work of both the Young Men's Christian Association (YMCA) and the Young Women's Christian Association (YWCA) to foster spiritual growth and character.[12] This change again mirrored transformations at White mainline Protestant institutions.

What made the HBCUs different from their White mainline counterparts was the tighter connection they had with African American churches. Drewry and Doermann provide a case study from Talladega that gives some sense of this involvement: "The year after the school opened, members of the college played an important part in establishing a Congregational Church in town. Two years later, the first Sunday school association was organized in the area. In the early 1870s, students from the theological department helped in the construction of twenty-five churches in Talladega and surrounding areas."[13] Of course, this involvement was not necessarily voluntary. For example, the 1896–97 catalog stipulated, "Students are required to attend punctually the following religious exercises: Church service and Sabbath school on the Sabbath, daily prayers at their boarding places, and in the morning at the chapel or school room. There are other services at which attendance is optional, although it is earnestly desired, and is very general. These are the services of the Missionary Societies, Mission Sabbath Schools, and Class and General Prayer Meetings."[14] In this respect, the cocurricular life of the HBCUs went hand in hand with the life of the African American churches.

Yet this close partnership also reflected an interesting challenge not faced in White institutions: the merging of African American and Christian identities. In particular, the challenge that emerged over the next century was whether the African American identity would eventually become more important than the Christian one—perhaps even becoming the sole core identity—for institutions trying to integrate and enhance both Christian and African American identities.

The close ties of HBCUs with African American churches did not prevent the similar liberalization that other mainline Protestant institutions underwent in the twentieth century. Some of this pressure came from the students themselves. For instance, in 1925, students rebelled against their strict rules at Fisk; meanwhile, Howard University students protested compulsory chapel.[15] Similar complaints occurred in the 1960s.[16]

So to what degree does the Christian foundation upon which these institutions were built still exist? Unfortunately, no one has studied the degree to which these kinds of movements or others had lasting influences on HBCUs. Although the story of Protestant institutions has been studied extensively, we lack a scholarly account of the Christian nature of many HBCUs.[17] Yet the importance of the Christian nature of these organizations for the African American community has long been understood as vital. Cassandra Chaney notes, "Religious organizations have been identified by many researchers to be the greatest institutions through which African Americans, individually and collectively, are spiritually, psychologically, emotionally, and physically enhanced."[18]

Thus, this chapter seeks to answer this question by examining both the Christian nature of the early legacy and the current state of the legacy regarding the Christian influence of the remaining forty-eight private four-year HBCUs still in existence today. It provides the first accounting of the current situation. It reveals that just as HBCUs imitated the trends of White mainline Protestant institutions regarding their early religious life, they have also imitated the secularization of these institutions, with only a few minor exceptions. Instead, the majority of private HBCUs have made the Black identity their core identity, thus marginalizing their Christian one. Today, most HBCUs prioritize African American empowerment over and above Christian theological and moral development. Indeed, in many cases—but not all—only traces of a Christian identity are apparent.

THE CHRISTIAN NATURE OF CONTEMPORARY HBCUs

Today ninety HBCUs fit our definition of a four-year university, and forty-eight of them are private. Yet of those forty-eight institutions, only thirty-five maintain discernible ties to their Christian heritage.[19] Over two-thirds of those thirty-five institutions only operationalize their Christian identity in minor ways (they score 6.5 or less on the Operationalizing Christian Identity Guide [OCIG]). Although one study has claimed the forty-eight private HBCUs "view IFL [the integration of faith and learning] as central to their mission," the reality is that the operationalized decisions of over two-thirds of these institutions do not support that claim.[20] Only nine HBCUs have any significant operationalization of the Christian mission (scoring 8 or more on the OCIG). Furthermore, only three score over 13.

THE ELITE PRIVATE HBCUs

One of the most obvious similarities to White mainline Protestant institutions is that the most prestigious Protestant HBCUs are all almost fully secularized. The *U.S. News & World Report* lists private Spelman College, Howard University, Morehouse College, Hampton University, Claflin University, and Fisk University as six of the top eleven HBCUs (the others are all state funded except for the Catholic Xavier University of Louisiana). All but one of these institutions demonstrate minimal marks of Christian commitment (3 or less).

At Howard University, Christianity no longer is favored, even on the official chapel page, although it should be noted that Howard is a special case of a "private" university, since it began with and still receives federal funding. Particularly surprising for an institution founded in the Baptist church, Morehouse has gone even further, including no mention of Christ on its website. This secularization is quite a departure from its early history, whose writer described the class in this way: "All were poor boys, working for eight cents an hour out-of-doors, on the halls, in the printing office or laundry, to help to pay the expense of board. A rough, sturdy Christian fellowship rang through all, and made them inseparably one."[21] One does find a historical mention of Christ in *Spelman College Student Handbook and Resource Guide*. It states, "The College Motto, embedded on the Spelman Scal, is 'Our Whole School for Christ.' It serves as a testament to the faith of the Founders. Though Spelman was founded in a basement of a Baptist church, there are no formal ties to any denomination, and it has always been open to women from all religious affiliations."[22] Indeed, one of the only other places where one finds mention of Christ is their voluntary chapel: "With a ministry that lies in the intersection of justice and the liberating power of the Gospel of Jesus Christ, Sisters Chapel is an interfaith, affirming, and extravagantly welcoming space to anyone in earnest search for spiritual rooting."[23] The whole school is no longer, as its motto once declared, "for Christ." Table 3.1 provides a glimpse into the degree to which most of these elite HBCUs operationalize their Christian identity at present. Given their distinctly Christian history, such trends contradicted our expectations, generally speaking, for these HBCUs (see Table 3.1).

Table 3.1. Elite Protestant Private HBCUs

U.S. News & World Report Rank and Name	Historical Denominational Tradition or Group	OCIG Score
1. Spelman College	American Baptist	2
2. Howard University	AMA	0
3. Xavier University of Louisiana	Catholic	11.5
4. Morehouse College	American Baptist	0
6. Hampton University	AMA	0
9. Clafin University	United Methodist	3
11. Fisk University	AMA	2

Only one exception warrants attention. Xavier University of Louisiana has combined the significant operationalization of its Catholic identity with academic achievement. It requires two theology courses for all students and integrates Christianity into the cocurriculum in a variety of ways.

LIMITED OPERATIONALIZATION OF CHRISTIAN IDENTITY AT HBCUs (1 TO 6.5)

Like most elite Protestant HBCUs, the majority of private HBCUs have few additional markers of the present influence of Christianity on administrative decision-making (see Table 3.2). Not one of these twenty-two institutions describes itself as Christian on the first page of its website, and only nine mention their church affiliation on their "About Us" pages. Moreover, only four affirm Christianity as central to their missions (Livingstone, Paul Quinn, Virginia University of Lynchburg, and Wiley), and one (Livingstone) has no other markers of a Christian identity. Similarly, only three institutions require a Christian course, and only one (Allen) uses any Christian reasoning in its student conduct code. Notably, not a single one of these institutions operationalizes its Christian identity in administrative decisions related to membership.

Table 3.2. HBCUs with Few Empirical Markers of Christian Influence

Institution Name	Denomination	OCIG Score
Benedict University	American Baptist	1
Tougaloo College	United Church of Christ	1
Bennett College	United Methodist	1.5
LeMoyne-Owen College	United Church of Christ	2
Livingstone College	AME Zion	2
Morris College	Baptist Educational & Missionary Convention of SC	2
Shaw University	American Baptist	2
Wilberforce University	AME	2
Huston-Tillotson University	United Methodist & United Church of Christ	2.5
Dillard University	United Methodist & United Church of Christ	3
Virginia University of Lynchburg	Baptist	3
Wiley College	United Methodist	3
Clinton College	AME	3.5
Rust College	United Methodist Episcopal	3.5
Allen University	AME	4

Table 3.2. HBCUs with Few Empirical Markers of Christian Influence (*continued*)

Institution Name	Denomination	OCIG Score
Texas College	Methodist Episcopal Church	4
Lane College	Christian Methodist Episcopal	4.5
Morris Brown College	AME	4.5
Virginia Union University	American Baptist	4.5
St. Augustine's College	Episcopal Church / Reformed	5.5
Philander Smith College	United Methodist	5.5
Paul Quinn College	AME	6

SIGNIFICANT OPERATIONALIZATION OF CHRISTIAN IDENTITY AT HBCUs (7 TO 22)

In addition to Xavier University of Louisiana, there is a group of ten other HBCUs that make significant efforts to operationalize the Christian identity of their institutions (see Table 3.3). All but one affirm the centrality of the Christian mission instead of only a church affiliation. Likewise, all but two require chapel attendance, all but three require a Christian course, and all but four mention Christianity in their conduct codes.

Table 3.3. HBCUs with Significant Empirical Markers of Christian Identity Influence

Institution Name	Denomination	OCIG Score
Paine College	United Methodist	7.5
Jarvis Christian College	Disciples of Christ	8
Bethune-Cookman University	United Methodist	8.5
Edward Waters University	AME	9
Voorhees College	Episcopal Church	9

Table 3.3. HBCUs with Significant Empirical Markers of Christian Identity Influence (*continued*)

Institution Name	Denomination	OCIG Score
Arkansas Baptist College	Missionary Baptist State Convention of Arkansas	10.5
Stillman College	Presbyterian USA	11
American Baptist College	American Baptist	14.5
Oakwood University	Seventh-day Adventist	18
Simmons College of Kentucky	General Association of Baptists in Kentucky	22

Still, only three HBCUs give high priority to operationalizing their Christian identity as we've measured it. Additionally, only one of these three has over one thousand students—Oakwood University (1,526). Given its size and serious operationalization of its Christian mission when evaluated according to the OCIG, we found it worthy of further consideration. A recent study of its professors found that they give attention to the Christian mission in four ways.[24] First, they seek to foster a connection or relationship with God that they then hope to similarly encourage among students. As one professor notes, "I have two goals as an integrator of faith and learning, to reflect the connection I have with Christ, and to help my students develop their connection with Him."[25] Second, they seek to model Christ's character. One professor notes, "I talk to my students about designing cost-effective medication for low-income families. . . . It goes back to serving the less fortunate as Christ did."[26] Third, they engage in spiritual disciplines with the students. Finally, students intersperse biblical content into their lessons. One faculty member shares, "In my class, I present a hypothetical problem, and then I have my students provide solutions using a Biblical perspective."[27] As one of us has found in other research on Christian institutions, these teaching activities comprise the core aspects of how teachers envision Christ animating students' learning.[28]

CONCLUSION

As our empirical overview reveals, HBCUs reflect the pattern of the White mainline Protestant approach to operationalizing their Christian identity. This reality should perhaps not be surprising, since almost all these existing HBCUs started between 1860 and 1900, the same time when many mainline Protestant institutions started. Not one HBCU has been started in the last one hundred years.

We do wonder if HBCUs that want to revive the operationalization of their Christian identity might benefit from looking to other models, such as the Catholic, evangelical, or Low Church models described in the rest of this book or even international models. For example, Christian higher education is growing the fastest of any place in the world in sub-Saharan Africa, where more Christian universities have started over the past two and half decades than in the rest of the world combined.[29] From a worldwide perspective, Black Christian higher education is growing and prospering like never before; however, HBCUs in the United States are currently not a part of that growth.

CHAPTER 4

Catholic Colleges and Universities

For the first 250 years of US higher education, Catholic institutions remained on the margins. In 1907, the undergraduate enrollment at Catholic colleges and universities totaled less than 9,800 students (less than 3 percent of total college enrollment at the time), and not one Catholic institution offered a doctoral degree.[1] Mainline Protestant institutions dominated the US higher education landscape.

Yet as mainline Protestant institutions secularized throughout the twentieth century, Catholic higher education in the United States burgeoned to achieve the dominance it now has among faith-based institutions in the United States.[2] In a little more than three decades (1907–40), Catholic enrollment swelled to 162,000 students at over two hundred colleges and universities, composing close to 11 percent of the total college enrollment.[3] Today, institutions fitting our definition of an undergraduate multidisciplinary Catholic college or university enroll over 650,000 students (compared to 191,000 for the mainline Protestants).

Although Catholic institutions have also struggled with modernity and the many factors encouraging them to disengage from their Catholic identity, unlike mainline Protestant universities, Catholic institutions throughout the twentieth century and today continue to maintain their Catholic identity and missions.

Authoritative Catholic social teaching has helped set forth a vision of Christian faithfulness in higher education. For instance, *Ex Corde Ecclesiae*, issued by John Paul II in 1990, promulgated a specific framework for how to maintain, preserve, and enhance the Catholic identity of higher education.[4] Since its passage, various scholars have conducted studies evaluating the Catholic identity of faculty, mission statements, vision statements, websites, and marketing strategies of Catholic institutions in the United States.[5] Our Operationalizing Christian Identity Guide (OCIG) combines an evaluation of all these independent factors into a single, cohesive tool for analyzing how that institutional identity is put into practice.

THE DIVERSITY WITHIN THE UNITY

One of the most noteworthy findings from our analysis of Catholic institutions is that virtually all of them still have significant identity markers of Catholicism. Unlike our study of mainline Protestant institutions or historically Black colleges and universities, we came across only a couple of formerly Catholic institutions that had secularized. Table 4.1 indicates the percentage of existing Catholic institutions we found to have various markers.

Table 4.1. Summary of Institutions Receiving Points by Decision-Making Category

Administrative Decision-Making Category	Total Institutions	Percentage of N
Voluntary but Privileged Mass	179	100
Mission Statement Mentions Catholic Mission	172	96
"About Us" Page Mentions Catholic Identity	149	83
Require President to Be Catholic	136	76
Only Christian Student Groups	128	72
Require Christian Courses (1+)	127	71

Table 4.1. Summary of Institutions Receiving Points by Decision-Making Category (*continued*)

Administrative Decision-Making Category	Total Institutions	Percentage of *N*
Christian Department	118	66
Require at Least Partial Catholic Membership for Board	112	63
Christian Centers or Institutes	99	55
VP for Mission	98	55
Code of Conduct Mentions Catholicism	83	46
Require Christian Courses (2+)	78	44
First Web Page Mentions Christian/Catholic Identity	64	36
Christian Reasoning or Covenant in Conduct Code	42	24
Require Christian Courses (3+)	34	19
Require Christian Courses (4+)	14	8
Require Catholic Membership for Faculty	9	5
Require Catholic Membership for Staff	8	5
Require Board to Be Catholic	5	3
Require Mass	2	1
Require Catholic Membership for Students	1	0.6

Note: N = 179.

As the table indicates, one of the major reasons no Catholic institutions score below 3.5 is that virtually all of them refer to their Catholic identity and their order identity (if applicable) in their mission statements (96 percent). Only two institutions do not mention either of these identities. Furthermore, all offer privileged Catholic mass on campus. Additionally, 83 percent of institutions affirm their Catholic identity in their "About Us" sections. Three-fourths of institutions explicitly require the president to be Catholic. Over two-thirds require a Christian course for all students (71 percent), and nearly three-fourths have only Christian religious groups among their student organizations on campus (72 percent).

Most Catholic institutions, however, do not require two or more Christian courses (44 percent require at least two), nor do they refer to Christian reasoning in their code of conduct (54 percent do not) or use Christian reasoning to justify any part of it (only 24 percent do). In addition, beyond the president, 5 percent or less require faculty or staff to be Catholic, and only one institution requires students to be Catholic. Although the OCIG reveals a broad continuum, we think it is helpful and possible to place institutions together in groups to aid understanding. Thus, we will describe the key characteristics of particular groupings of Catholic institutions.

MINIMAL CATHOLIC UNIVERSITIES: MISSION, IDENTITY, AND MASS

Due to the lack of secularization among Catholic institutions, the presence of privileged mass at every institution, and reference to the Catholic and/or order identity in 96 percent of statements, only three Catholic institutions score below 5 on our scale (College of Saint Rose, Spalding University, and Mount Saint Joseph), and only fourteen score 6.5 or below (see Table 4.2). We call these "minimal Catholic universities." The reason is that these institutions do not have many empirical markers beyond those already mentioned. For example, only one requires a religion course related to Christianity, not one has a theology rather than a religious studies department, only two mention the Catholic identity on the opening web page, only two have a vice president for mission, and two have Christian centers. Finally, not one institution scoring 6.5 or below mentions the Catholic tradition in its code of conduct or uses Catholic moral reasoning in the code.

Table 4.2. Minimal Catholic Universities

Institution Name	OCIG Score
College of Saint Rose	3.5
Spalding University	3.5
Mount Saint Joseph	4.5
Christian Brothers University	5.5
Clarke University	5.5
Mount Saint Mary's University (CA)	5.5
Notre Dame de Namur University	5.5
D'Youville College	6
Misericordia University	6
Chestnut Hill College	6.5
College of Mount Saint Vincent	6.5
Felician University	6.5
Mercy College of Ohio	6.5
Ursuline College	6.5

BASIC CATHOLIC UNIVERSITIES:
ADDING CHRISTIAN ETHOS AND GOVERNANCE

Institutions scoring from 7 to 8 (twenty-seven universities) have operationalized significant elements related to their Catholic identity. The major additions compared to the minimal Catholic institutions involve the rhetoric on the "About Us" page (67 percent mention a Catholic identity), governance (78 percent require at least some board members to be Catholic), and the percentage that only has a Christian student group on campus (67 percent). In addition, 44 percent have a vice president for mission. Thus, we label this group as "basic Catholic universities" (see Table 4.3).

Table 4.3. Basic Catholic Universities

Institution Name	OCIG Score
Cabrini University	7
Edgewood College	7
Fontbonne University	7
Mount Mercy College	7
Quincy University	7
Rosemont College of the Holy Child Jesus	7
Saint Mary-of-the-Woods College	7
Saint Thomas Aquinas College	7
Siena Heights University	7
Albertus Magnus College	7.5
Alverno College	7.5
De Paul University	7.5
Maria College	7.5
Saint Martin's University	7.5
Saint Xavier University	7.5
Dominican College of Blauvelt	8
Georgian Court University	8
Gwynedd-Mercy University	8
La Salle University	8
Loyola University New Orleans	8
Manor College	8
Merrimack College	8
Mount Saint Mary College	8
Regis College	8
Saint Edward's University	8
Saint Louis University	8
University of Saint Mary	8

Among basic Catholic universities, only a minority of the institutions have a specifically Christian academic department (33 percent), require a Christian course (19 percent), have Christian centers (22 percent), or describe their identity as Catholic on their initial web pages (26 percent).

CATHOLIC CURRICULAR UNIVERSITIES

The next grouping of Catholic colleges and universities scores between 8.5 and 10 (forty-nine institutions). These institutions share the basic characteristics of previous groupings but gain additional points primarily through their curricular and research decisions. While increasingly demonstrating some of the distinctives already noted, the most important changes are that most of these institutions require a Christian course for all students (69 percent), have Catholic institutions or centers on campus (59 percent), and host a Christian theology department (51 percent). Consequently, we call these institutions "Catholic curricular universities" (Table 4.4).

Table 4.4. Catholic Curricular Universities

Institution Name	OCIG Score
Avila University	8.5
Bellarmine University	8.5
College of Our Lady of the Elms	8.5
Georgetown University	8.5
John Carroll University	8.5
Sacred Heart University	8.5
Saint Elizabeth University	8.5
Seattle University	8.5
Trinity University	8.5
University of Saint Joseph	8.5
Carlow University	9
Donnelly College	9
Duquesne University	9
Fordham University	9
Madonna University	9
Manhattan College	9
Molloy University	9
Mount Aloysius College	9

Table 4.4. Catholic Curricular Universities (*continued*)

Institution Name	OCIG Score
Saint Ambrose University	9
St. Francis University	9
University of Holy Cross	9
University of San Diego	9
University of San Francisco	9
College of the Holy Cross	9.5
Iona College	9.5
Le Moyne College	9.5
Marywood University	9.5
Neumann University	9.5
Notre Dame College	9.5
Rockhurst University	9.5
Saint Michael's College	9.5
University of Saint Francis (IN)	9.5
University of the Incarnate Word	9.5
Villa Maria College	9.5
Aquinas College (MI)	10
Calumet College of St. Joseph	10
College of Saint Mary	10
Fairfield University	10
Hilbert College	10
La Roche University	10
Loras College	10
Loyola University Chicago	10
Niagara University	10
Rivier University	10
Saint Mary's College of California	10
Siena College	10
University of Detroit Mercy	10
Walsh University	10
Wheeling Jesuit University	10

A substantial minority of institutions in this group also have a vice president for mission (49 percent) and mention the Catholic mission in the code of conduct (39 percent). That being said, these institutions are still shy about their Catholic identity on their initial web pages (only 22 percent mention it).

GENERAL CATHOLIC UNIVERSITIES

The forty-two institutions that score between 10.5 and 12 points show a greater Catholic presence regarding most standards outside of membership. Therefore, we call them "general Catholic universities" (Table 4.5). For example, all but two have a Christian curricular requirement, and 60 percent require more than one Christian course. In addition, 88 percent have theology departments instead of religious studies departments. Perhaps the key distinguishing feature of these institutions is related to governance. Almost three-fourths (74 percent) have a vice president for mission, and almost two-thirds indicate they have a Catholic requirement for at least some board members. In addition, 55 percent have a Christian center or institute.

Table 4.5. General Catholic Universities

Institution Name	OCIG Score
Anna Maria College	10.5
College of St. Catherine	10.5
Franciscan Missionaries of Our Lady University	10.5
Immaculata University	10.5
Marian University	10.5
Our Lady of the Lake University	10.5
Salve Regina University	10.5
Seton Hill University	10.5
Spring Hill College	10.5
Viterbo University	10.5
Benedictine University	11

Table 4.5. General Catholic Universities (*continued*)

Institution Name	OCIG Score
Chaminade University of Honolulu	11
College of Saint Scholastica	11
Gannon University	11
Holy Family University	11
Marquette University	11
Mercyhurst University	11
Saint Bonaventure University	11
Seton Hall University	11
University of Saint Francis (IL)	11
University of Saint Thomas (MN)	11
Brescia University	11.5
Canisius College	11.5
College of Saint Benedict	11.5
Mount Marty College	11.5
Regis University	11.5
Saint Joseph's University	11.5
Saint Mary's College	11.5
Saint Peter's University	11.5
Xavier University of Louisiana	11.5
Alvernia University	12
Gonzaga University	12
Lewis University	12
Lourdes College	12
Marian University	12
Mount Mary College	12
Ohio Dominican University	12
Saint Joseph's College	12
Saint Mary's University	12
Stonehill College	12
University of Dallas	12
University of Saint Thomas (TX)	12

Despite a distinctly Christian approach in several categories, the codes of conduct for these institutions remain largely secular. Although half mention Catholicism or Christianity in the code (52 percent), only around 17 percent use Christian reasoning to defend at least some portion of the code. In addition, none of these institutions have additional faculty or staff Christian membership requirements beyond the above 50 percent number prescribed by *Ex Corde*.

ROBUST CATHOLIC UNIVERSITIES

Institutions in the 12.5–14 ranking (thirty-four total) share several markers (see Table 4.6). All have clear Catholic missions, and all but one identify as Catholic on their "About Us" pages. A significant minority (47 percent) even identify as Catholic on their introductory web pages. The curricular investment in the Catholic mission is pervasive. All have a theology department and require at least one Christian course, with 91 percent requiring at least two. Eighty-eight percent of the institutions have a Catholic institute or center, and 68 percent have a vice president for mission. In the cocurriculum, 79 percent have exclusively Christian student religious groups, and 71 percent mention Catholicism in the code of conduct.

Table 4.6. Robust Catholic Universities

Institution Name	OCIG Score
Barry University	12.5
Briar Cliff University	12.5
Loyola University Maryland	12.5
Loyola Marymount University	12.5
Marymount University	12.5
Newman University	12.5
University of Mary	12.5
Assumption University	13
Dominican University	13

Table 4.6. Robust Catholic Universities (*continued*)

Institution Name	OCIG Score
Mount St. Mary's University (MD)	13
Saint Anselm College	13
Saint John's University	13
Saint Norbert College	13
University of Dayton	13
University of Portland	13
University of Providence	13
University of Scranton	13
Xavier University	13
Aquinas College (TN)	13.5
Belmont Abbey College	13.5
Boston College	13.5
Caldwell University	13.5
DeSales University	13.5
King's College	13.5
Saint Thomas University	13.5
Saint Vincent College	13.5
Creighton University	14
Emmanuel College	14
Providence College	14
Saint John's University	14
Saint Leo University	14
Saint Mary's University	14
Santa Clara University	14
The Catholic University of America	14

These institutions remain relatively open, however, in that only 3 percent have Catholic requirements for faculty or staff beyond those in *Ex Corde*. Finally, less than half (47 percent) use Christian reasoning in their student code of conduct.

COMPREHENSIVE CATHOLIC UNIVERSITIES

Thirteen institutions score in the range of 15 to 23 (see Table 4.7). Fascinatingly, only 38 percent of these highest-scoring institutions are associated with a specific Catholic order. In contrast, 93 percent of the Catholic universities in the other score categories are affiliated with an order. Overall, institutions in this category make decisions regarding membership, curriculum, cocurriculum, and governance that are distinct from the rest of their peers. We found that it is unusual for a Catholic institution to require faculty and staff to be Catholic, yet 62 percent of institutions within this category have such a requirement.

In the curricular domain, all these institutions have theology departments and require numerous courses on Christianity (92 percent require three or more). In cocurricular decisions, 69 percent explicitly require that Christian/Catholic standards be followed in student life, and 85 percent have exclusively Christian student religious groups. Furthermore, 69 percent have Christian centers or institutions.

Table 4.7. Comprehensive Catholic Universities

Institution Name	OCIG Score
Carroll College	15
Villanova University	15
Thomas More University	15.5
University of Notre Dame	15.5
Ave Maria University	16
Franciscan University	16
Benedictine College	16.5
Thomas More College of Liberal Arts	18.5
Thomas Aquinas College	19
Magdalen College	19.5
Christendom College	20.5
Wyoming Catholic College	20.5
John Paul the Great Catholic University	23

CONCLUSION

Overall, Catholic universities demonstrate tremendous variety in how they operationalize their identity. As we will show in Chapter Eight, however, the majority tend to score between 5 and 15, which is a sharp contrast to the different Protestant approaches. Catholic universities, perhaps because of their long history stretching back to the start of universities, tend to create fewer Christian membership boundaries and also draw on the Christian identity for operationalization in both the curriculum and cocurriculum.

Yet important changes are happening in Catholic higher education. We found the most recent Catholic institution started by an order is Neumann University, which originated in 1965. In contrast, the seven Catholic institutions started since that time all score above 17 on the OCIG, but not one of them was started by an order. It appears future expansion of Catholic higher education will not be initiated by orders. Furthermore, our findings clarify that the laypeople starting these institutions want them to be comprehensively and distinctively Catholic. A recent book on the future of Catholic higher education mentions the importance of lay leadership, and our empirical findings reveal that its importance warrants further emphasis.[6]

We suggest this finding may indicate future clashes between the educational vision of conservative laity and the leaders of shrinking Catholic orders. Educational leaders from the orders may interpret emphasis upon maintaining a distinctive Catholic identity as creating more Catholic institutions focused solely on the good of the Catholic Church versus serving the common good and broader public. Yet conservative laity may see the necessity of these changes because of a shift in strategy amid a post-Christian culture. They perceive that the hostile culture of higher education requires institutions that maintain the educational mission and faithfulness of the Catholic Church in more distinct ways.

CHAPTER 5

Evangelical Colleges and Universities in Multidenominational Coalitions

Historically, Evangelicals have been known for their focus on the importance of Christ and Christ's death and resurrection, conversion, biblical authority, and social action.[1] They are also known for creating multidenominational partnerships based on these shared theological beliefs, such as the National Association of Evangelicals (NAE). The same has also been true for colleges and universities over the past half century. The two largest partnerships of evangelical institutions today are the Council for Christian Colleges and Universities (CCCU) and the International Alliance for Christian Education (IACE). Each of the organizations has certain requirements that automatically place their institutions within a certain score on the Operationalizing Christian Identity Guide (OCIG). In fact, of all the groups of faith-based institutions, the evangelical colleges and universities that compose the CCCU and IACE are the most committed to operationalizing the Christian mission in their institutions.

THE CCCU

The CCCU originated in 1976 as a result of the partnership between the Commission on Higher Education of the NAE and the Christian College Consortium (a key forerunner of the CCCU).[2] Today, the CCCU includes 188 institutions around the world. One hundred and thirty-four of those institutions meet our definition of a multidisciplinary college or university located in the United States (another eight that meet our definition are located in Canada and will be covered in Chapter Ten).

The CCCU institutions in the United States prioritize their faith in common ways, and as a result, each scores 12 or above on the OCIG. First, every CCCU school has a strong Christian mission and proclaims its connection to Christianity or a Christian denomination on its "About Us" page. Second, every institution requires the president and the governing board to be Christian. Third, all but one CCCU college or university privileges Christian chapel, and 87 percent require chapel attendance. Fourth, all CCCU institutions require one Christian course, and 95 percent require two or more. Finally, 90 percent use Christian reasoning in their conduct codes, and 90 percent only have Christian student groups on their campuses. Overall, these institutions operationalize their Christian identity in significant ways.

Still, there are a few important differences among CCCU institutions. Some of those differences are recognized by distinguishing categories created by the CCCU, which divides its member schools according to these categories: collaborative partners, associate members, and governing members. In what follows, we will unpack the key OCIG markers of those CCCU membership differences and patterns across CCCU schools that admit non-Christian and only Christian students, and we will also explore the IACE schools.

Collaborative Partners

To be a governing or associate member of the CCCU, an institution must have an employment policy that they "hire as full-time faculty members and administrators only persons who profess faith in Jesus Christ."[3]

Institutions identified as collaborative partners do not necessarily have that policy, so they are categorized differently.

Since they either do not require all faculty, staff, or administrators to be Christian or depart in other ways from CCCU norms, this group, within the larger population of CCCU institutions, tends to have lower OCIG scores (see Table 5.1). For instance, half of the institutions do not require staff to be Christian, and almost all of them do not require more than three Christian courses (Whitworth University is the exception in that it requires five). None require students to be Christian. Baylor University and Pepperdine University received two of the lowest scores because they do not use Christian reasoning in their student conduct codes and do not have specific Christian academic departments.

Table 5.1. OCIG Scores of CCCU Collaborative Partners

Institution Name	OCIG Score
Campbell University	12
Baylor University	13
Pepperdine University	13
Samford University	15
Friends University	17
Warner Pacific College	17
Seattle Pacific University	18
Whitworth University	20

Governing and Associate Members

The rest of the CCCU membership is composed of governing and associate members—almost all of whom score 14 or more on the OCIG (only 2 percent do not). Governing members are comprehensive multidisciplinary institutions that meet our definition of a college or university and are accredited. Every institution requires Christian membership for faculty, board, and administrative leadership; espouses a Christian mission; identifies as Christian on their "About Us" page; and requires at least one Christian course.[4] In addition, 89 percent market themselves on their home pages as Christian. Both groups, through either department names (95 percent) or required courses (96 percent require over two Christian courses), operationalize their Christian identity in the curricula. Furthermore, in the cocurriculum, 92 percent use Christian reasoning in their conduct codes, and 89 percent make chapel mandatory. Table 5.2 provides an overview of the high percentage of the 127 CCCU governing and associate members possessing various OCIG characteristics.

Table 5.2. Summary of Institutions Receiving Points by Decision-Making Category

Administrative Decision-Making Category	Percentage of N
Mission Statement Mentions Christian Mission	100
Require Faculty, Board & President to Be Christian	100
Require Christian Courses (1+)	100
Staff Required to Be Christian	100
"About Us" Page Mentions Christian Identity	100
Require Christian Courses (2+)	96
Christian Department	95
Christian Covenant or Christian Reasoning in Conduct Code	92
Only Christian Student Groups	90
Home Page Mentions Christian Identity	89
Require Chapel	89
Require Christian Courses (3+)	66
Require Christian Courses (4+)	47
Students Required to Be Christian	29
Require Christian Courses (5+)	27
Christian Covenant for Students	25
VP for Mission / Chaplain on Executive Leadership Team	18
Christian Centers or Institutes	14

Note: N = 126.

As one can see from Table 5.2, the major institutional differences pertain to the number of courses they require (66 percent require three or more, 47 percent require four or more, and 27 percent require five or more), the requirement that students be Christian (29 percent), the presence of a Christian covenant (25 percent), the presence of a vice president for mission or chaplain on the executive leadership team (18 percent), and the sponsorship of Christian centers or institutions (14 percent).

As we analyzed the data, we found that how institutions made decisions in these categories was contingent on whether they required students to be Christian. Institutions that had this requirement tended to score slightly higher (ranging between 17 and 26), and institutions that admitted non-Christian students tended to score slightly lower (ranging between 13 and 21). It should not be surprising that the vast majority of CCCU institutions (over 70 percent) admit non-Christians, since this policy allows them to reach a wider audience, both boosting enrollment and their ability to reach non-Christian students.

Admit Non-Christian Students

Despite the widespread practice of admitting non-Christian students, CCCU institutions in this category still varied greatly and can be subdivided even further based on four additional markers: those without three or more Christian courses, Christian requirements for students, a Christian community covenant for students, or a vice president for mission on the executive leadership team. Institutions in the first group (Table 5.3) do not have any of these additional markers. These institutions all score between 13 and 17.

Table 5.3. CCCU Governing Members *without* 3+ Christian Courses, Christian Requirements for Students, Christian Covenant, or VP for Mission

Institution Name	OCIG Score
Central Christian College	13
Bethany Lutheran College	14
Campbellsville University	14
Concordia University (IL)	14
Roberts Wesleyan College	14
University of the Southwest	14
Anderson University (IN)	15
Bethel University (IN)	15
Bluefield University	15
Concordia University (NE)	15
East Texas Baptist University	15
King University	15
Oklahoma Baptist University (CCCU & IACE)	15
Olivet Nazarene University	15
Ouachita Baptist University	15
Charleston Southern University	16
College of the Ozarks (CCCU & IACE)	16
Concordia University (CA)	16
Concordia University (MI)	16
Dallas Baptist University (CCCU & IACE)	16
Greenville University	16
Hannibal-LaGrange College (CCCU & IACE)	16
Hardin Simmons University	16
Howard Payne University (CCCU & IACE)	16
Judson University	16
Mississippi College	16
Missouri Baptist University (CCCU & IACE)	16
University of Mary Hardin-Baylor (CCCU & IACE)	16

Table 5.3. CCCU Governing Members *without* 3+ Christian Courses, Christian Requirements for Students, Christian Covenant, or VP for Mission (*continued*)

Institution Name	OCIG Score
Warner University	16
Wayland Baptist University (CCCU & IACE)	16
Concordia University (WI)	17
Houston Christian University (CCCU & IACE)	17
Southwest Baptist University (CCCU & IACE)	17

The institutions in Table 5.4 also do not require students to be Christian, but they have one or more of the additional empirical markers the institutions in Table 5.3 lacked. The result was an overall higher average score and a higher score range (13–22).

Table 5.4. CCCU Governing Members *without* Christian Requirements for Students but with Either Christian Covenant, VP for Mission, or 3+ Christian Required Courses

Institution Name	Required Christian Courses	VP for Mission	Covenant	OCIG Score
Los Angeles Pacific University	3	No	No	13
Erskine College (CCCU & IACE)	3	No	No	15
Milligan University	3	No	No	15
Mount Vernon Nazarene University	2	No	Yes	15
Oral Roberts University	2	No	Yes	15
Palm Beach Atlantic University	2	Yes	No	15
Bethel University (MN)	3	No	Yes	16
California Baptist University (CCCU & IACE)	3	No	No	16
Eastern Nazarene College	3	No	Yes	16
Fresno Pacific University	2	Yes	No	16
Geneva College (CCCU & IACE)	3	No	No	16
North Park University	2	Yes	No	16

Table 5.4. CCCU Governing Members *without* Christian Requirements for Students but with Either Christian Covenant, VP for Mission, or 3+ Christian Required Courses (*continued*)

Institution Name	Required Christian Courses	VP for Mission	Covenant	OCIG Score
Oklahoma Christian University	2	No	Yes	16
Southern Nazarene University (CCCU & IACE)	2	No	Yes	16
Southern Wesleyan University	3	No	Yes	16
Wisconsin Lutheran College (CCCU & IACE)	4	No	No	16
Anderson University (SC) (CCCU & IACE)	2	Yes	No	17
Calvin University	3	Yes	No	17
Central Baptist College	3	No	No	17
Hope International University	3	No	No	17
Lipscomb University	3	No	No	17
Mid-America Christian University	4	No	Yes	17
MidAmerica Nazarene University	3	No	No	17
Ohio Christian University	3	No	No	17
Regent University	3	No	No	17
Trinity Christian College	4	No	No	17
Asbury University	4	No	No	18
Belhaven College	5	No	No	18
Bushnell University	5	No	No	18
Emmanuel College (GA)	4	No	No	18
Harding University	4	No	No	18
Houghton University	3	Yes	No	18
Huntington University	3	Yes	No	18
John Brown University	4	No	Yes	18
Lee University	4	No	Yes	18
Lubbock Christian University	4	No	No	18
Malone University	4	No	No	18

Table 5.4. CCCU Governing Members *without* Christian Requirements for Students but with Either Christian Covenant, VP for Mission, or 3+ Christian Required Courses (*continued*)

Institution Name	Required Christian Courses	VP for Mission	Covenant	OCIG Score
Messiah University	4	No	Yes	18
Northwestern College (IA)	4	Yes	No	18
Point Loma Nazarene University	3	Yes	No	18
Point University (CCCU & IACE)	5	No	Yes	18
Simpson University (CA)	4	Yes	No	18
Southern Adventist University	4	Yes	No	18
Trinity International University	4	No	No	18
Walla Walla University	4	Yes	No	18
Westmont College	5	No	No	18
York University	4	No	No	18
Abilene Christian University	5	No	No	19
George Fox University	5	No	Yes	19
Indiana Wesleyan University	3	Yes	No	19
Kentucky Christian University	6	No	No	19
Northwest Nazarene University	4	Yes	Yes	19
Trevecca Nazarene University	5	No	No	19
Azusa Pacific University	5	No	No	20
Faulkner University	6	No	No	20
Montreat College	6	No	No	20
William Jessup University (CCCU & IACE)	7	No	Yes	21

Admit Only Christian Students

Admitting only Christians is a bold move that cuts an institution off from a supply of students it may need to survive. Thus, virtually all the institutions that only admit Christians enroll less than 2,500 undergraduates—Biola University, Colorado Christian University, LeTourneau University, University of Northwestern-St. Paul, and Southeastern University are exceptions.

As one would expect of institutions that choose to admit only Christian students, they score much higher on our OCIG measure (between 17 and 26) and have many of the other empirical markers not found as pervasively on campuses that admit non-Christians. Thus, instead of dividing these institutions, we have simply listed whether they have vice presidents for mission and community covenants alongside their OCIG scores (see Table 5.5).

Table 5.5. CCCU Governing Members Who Require Students to Be Christian

Institution Name	Required Christian Courses	VP for Mission	Covenant	OCIG Score
Evangel University	2	No	Yes	17
Sterling College	2	No	No	17
Dordt University (CCCU & IACE)	4	No	No	18
Gordon College	3	No	No	18
Spring Arbor University (CCCU & IACE)	3	No	Yes	18
Tabor College	3	No	Yes	18
Colorado Christian University (CCCU & IACE)	4	No	Yes	19
Corban University (CCCU & IACE)	4	No	No	19
Cornerstone University	3	Yes	Yes	19
LeTourneau University (CCCU & IACE)	4	No	Yes	19
Northwest University	4	No	No	19
San Diego Christian College (CCCU & IACE)	4	No	Yes	19
Southwestern Christian University	4	No	Yes	19
Grace College (CCCU & IACE)	3	Yes	No	20
Toccoa Falls College	5	No	Yes	20
University of Valley Forge	5	No	No	20
Vanguard University	5	No	No	20

Table 5.5. CCCU Governing Members Who Require Students to Be Christian (*continued*)

Institution Name	Required Christian Courses	VP for Mission	Covenant	OCIG Score
Alliance University	5	Yes	No	21
Columbia International University	6	No	No	21
Covenant College	5	Yes	No	21
Johnson University (FL)	5	No	No	21
Multnomah University	6	No	No	21
Arizona Christian University (CCCU & IACE)	6	No	No	22
Kuyper College	7	No	No	22
North Central University	6	Yes	No	22
Taylor University	6	Yes	Yes	22
University of Northwestern-St. Paul	7	No	Yes	22
Wheaton College	6	No	Yes	22
Mid-Atlantic Christian University	8	No	No	23
Southeastern University	6	Yes	Yes	23
Crown College	8	Yes	Yes	24
Cairn University (CCCU & IACE)	10	No	Yes	25
Clarks Summit University	10	No	No	25
Life Pacific University (CA)	10	No	No	25
Ozark Christian College	10	No	Yes	25
Biola University (CCCU & IACE)	10	No	No	26

INTERNATIONAL ALLIANCE FOR CHRISTIAN EDUCATION (IACE) UNIVERSITIES

IACE emerged out of a 2015 controversy within the CCCU about policies regarding same-sex marriage.[5] Two CCCU members, Eastern Mennonite University and Goshen College, had made the administrative decision to allow faculty and staff to be in same-sex marriages. The ensuing controversy resulted in two other institutions, Union University and Oklahoma Wesleyan University, leaving the CCCU in protest. Rather than cause further division, Eastern Mennonite and Goshen College also left the CCCU.

Although a major crisis within the CCCU was averted, dissatisfaction with how the matter was resolved led other institutions, particularly those associated with various Baptist state conventions in the South, to start their own organization known as IACE. The membership requirements are similar to CCCU institutions except that IACE adds this important addition: "Cultural Witness—IACE institutions and partners will seek to reflect a faithful Christian witness that reflects commitments to biblical orthodoxy and historic Christian teachings regarding cultural engagement and renewal of foundational social order, including marriage and family."[6] Currently, the IACE membership contains forty-three institutions that meet our definition of a multidisciplinary college or university.[7] Only fifteen of those are not part of the CCCU. Thus, Table 5.6 lists the scores of those fifteen members that are not affiliated with the CCCU.

Table 5.6. IACE Members Not Affiliated with the CCCU

Institution Name	Required Christian Courses	Student Required to be Christian	Covenant	OCIG Score
Blue Mountain College	2	No	No	15
New Saint Andrews	2	Yes	Yes	15
North Greenville University	2	No	No	15
Williams Baptist College	2	No	No	15
Louisiana Christian University	2	No	No	16
Carson-Newman University	2	No	No	17
Union University	2	No	Yes	17
Patrick Henry College	3	Yes	Yes	18
Bryan College	5	No	Yes	19

Table 5.6. IACE Members Not Affiliated with the CCCU (*continued*)

Institution Name	Required Christian Courses	Student Required to be Christian	Covenant	OCIG Score
Cedarville University	5	Yes	Yes	21
Criswell College	6	Yes	No	21
Grace Christian University	6	Yes	No	21
Providence Christian College	6	Yes	No	21
Welch College	10	No	No	22
Montana Christian College	10	Yes	Yes	25

As can be seen in the table, these IACE universities demonstrate the same variability in OCIG scores as CCCU institutions, with the majority scoring between 15 and 21. The major difference is that those scoring 21 or more require five or more Christian courses. In addition, as seen in the list of institutions that are both IACE and CCCU members (Table 5.7), there are no major score differences between institutions that are members of both organizations and those that are not.

Table 5.7. IACE Members Affiliated with the CCCU

Institution Name	Required Christian Courses	Students Required to be Christian	Covenant	OCIG Score
Erskine College	3	No	No	15
Oklahoma Baptist University	2	No	No	15
College of the Ozarks	2	No	No	16
California Baptist University	3	No	No	16
Dallas Baptist University	2	No	No	16
Geneva College	3	No	No	16
Hannibal-LaGrange College	2	No	No	16
Howard Payne University	2	No	No	16

Table 5.7. IACE Members Affiliated with the CCCU (*continued*)

Institution Name	Required Christian Courses	Students Required to be Christian	Covenant	OCIG Score
Missouri Baptist University	2	No	No	16
Southern Nazarene University	2	No	Yes	16
University of Mary Hardin-Baylor	2	No	No	16
Wayland Baptist University	2	No	No	16
Wisconsin Lutheran College	2	Yes	No	16
Anderson University (SC)	2	Yes	No	17
Houston Christian University	2	No	No	17
Southwest Baptist University	2	Yes	No	17
Dordt University	4	Yes	No	18
Point University	5	Yes	Yes	18
Spring Arbor University	3	Yes	Yes	18
Colorado Christian University	4	Yes	Yes	19
Corban University	4	Yes	No	19
LeTourneau University	4	Yes	Yes	19
San Diego Christian College	4	Yes	Yes	19
Grace College	3	Yes	No	20
Arizona Christian University	6	Yes	No	22
William Jessup University	7	Yes	Yes	21
Cairn University	10	Yes	Yes	25
Biola University	10	Yes	No	26

CONCLUSION

As made clear in this chapter, leaders at institutions affiliated with the CCCU and/or the IACE can be counted on to establish structures that confidently reflect the Christian identity espoused by their institutional missions. The Christian commitment required for key leadership positions—and, for the most part, faculty and staff as well—has led these institutions to express their faith in structures across their campuses to a greater degree (on the whole) than any other grouping we discuss in this book. The minimum score from this group (12) is significantly higher than the minimum score from mainline Protestants (1), historically Black colleges and universities (1), Catholic institutions (3.5), and independent Low Church Protestants (4). The self-selection into an organization like the CCCU or the IACE results in a relatively homogenous grouping of institutions (with regard to OCIG scores). Even despite the different philosophies motivating or prohibiting the admission of non-Christians, in the end, CCCU and IACE institutions demonstrate that both types of campuses can maintain and embody the distinctiveness of their Christian missions.

CHAPTER 6

Independent Low Church Protestant Colleges and Universities

The most distinctive and wide-ranking Christian institutions in the field of faith-based higher education, according to our Operationalizing Christian Identity Guide (OCIG), are independent Low Church Protestant institutions. The designation of "Low Church" stands in contrast to the formality of the "High Church" traditions. Low Church traditions do not have pastors with collars or official clothing, do not use incense and chant, and do not typically practice infant baptism. The sixty-two institutions we designated as Low Church Protestants are affiliated with Baptist, Churches of Christ, Mennonite, nondenominational/multidenominational, and Seventh-day Adventist traditions.[1] Their institutional characteristics according to the OCIG are the exact opposite of mainline Protestant institutions. Fifty-three (86 percent of Low Church schools) score 10 or above, and only nine score less than 10. Almost all are countercultural when it comes to the secular norms of how to run and organize universities in that they are likely to transform numerous secular administrative standards regarding things like hiring or curriculum using their Christian identity and criteria.

These institutions are also countercultural in other ways: their academic culture (e.g., many are theologically conservative), their Christian theological beliefs (e.g., eleven institutions embrace pacifism), or simply their place among influential US religious life (not one of these institutions represents the powerful mainline Protestant denominations, and their denominations do not represent the highest-earning socioeconomic groups in the United States).

And there are other distinctives to this group. Some have to do with their varied sizes. This group contains the two largest Christian universities in the world (Grand Canyon and Liberty University) and thirty-three institutions with total enrollments below one thousand students. The institutions also span the theological and political spectrum—from the highly conservative Bob Jones University and Liberty to the more progressive Mennonite USA and Baptist campuses such as Belmont University, Bluffton University, and Goshen College, as well as various campuses in between. Their diversity is, in many respects, a product of their independence—a type of independence that is only found in the United States.

THE INDEPENDENT LOW CHURCH OUTLIERS

The nine Low Church Protestant outliers that score 8 or below (see Table 6.1) all have either a Baptist, Mennonite, or nondenominational identity. Three have other identities that take precedence over their Christian one. For instance, Hillsdale College is known more for its political conservativism than its Christian identity, and likewise, Berea College is best known for being one of the first colleges in which students work for their tuition. Amberton University is strictly an online university for working adults. Only one of these outliers restricts the hiring of faculty or staff to Christians (Amberton), and only two require a Christian course (Berea and Wingate). We anticipate that most of these institutions will continue to drift toward secularization in the coming decades.

Table 6.1. Independent Low Church Outliers

Institution Name	Year Founded	OCIG Score
Limestone University	1845	4
Wingate University	1896	4
Berry College	1902	5
Bethel College (KS)	1887	5.5
Hillsdale College	1844	6
Berea College	1855	7
Mars Hill University	1856	7
Amberton University	1971	8
University of Mount Olive	1951	8

SIGNIFICANT BUT NOT PERVASIVE OPERATIONALIZATION OF THE CHRISTIAN IDENTITY

The next fifteen colleges, scoring between 10 and 14.5 (see Table 6.2), come from a wider array of traditions, such as Adventist, Baptist, Mennonite, and nondenominational. They include nine institutions with less than one thousand students, as well as two of the top five largest Christian universities (Grand Canyon University and University of the Cumberlands). What makes this group different from the earlier group is that all but one (University of Fort Lauderdale) require at least one course related to Christianity, and all of them offer a Christian chapel (attendance is required on eight campuses). In addition, two-thirds (ten) require faculty to be Christian. Yet in various ways, some also downplay their Christian missions. Seven of them do not identify as Christian on their initial home pages, and a different seven have generic religion departments.

Table 6.2. Significant but Not Pervasive Operationalization of the Christian Identity

Institution Name	Required Christian Courses	Home Page Christian Identity	Christian Reasoning in Student Code	OCIG Score
Chowan University	1	Yes	No	10
Washington Adventist University	1	No	Yes	10
Georgetown College	1	Yes	Yes	10.5
University of the Cumberlands	1	No	No	11
William Carey University	2	No	Yes	11.5
Oakland City University	1	Yes	Yes	12.5
Carolina University	2	No	No	13
Goshen University	1	Yes	Yes	13
University of Fort Lauderdale	0	Yes	Yes	13
Gardner-Webb University	3	Yes	No	13.5
Brewton-Parker College	2	No	Yes	14
Hesston College	1	Yes	Yes	14
Shorter University (GA)	3	No	Yes	14
Union College	4	No	No	14
Grand Canyon University	2	Yes	Yes	14.5

PERVASIVE OPERATIONALIZATION OF THE CHRISTIAN IDENTITY

Sixty-one percent of all the Low Church countercultural group score 15 or above on the OCIG. Table 6.3 provides insight into how pervasive the operationalization of the Christian identity is at these institutions for particular markers. As can be seen, over 90 percent operationalize their Christian identity regarding ten of the markers. The major differences have to do with the number of Christian courses required, marketing, Christian reasoning in the student conduct code, and membership requirements for students.

Table 6.3. Key Markers of Pervasive Operationalization in Low Church
Institutions

Administrative Distinctive	%
Require President to Be Christian	100
Require Christian Courses (1+)	100
Require Christian Courses (2+)	100
Christian Mission	97
"About Us" Page Mentions Christian Identity	97
Privilege Christian Worship	97
Require Faculty to Be Christian	95
Require Staff to Be Christian	92
Christian Department	90
First Web Page Mentions Christian Identity	90
Require Christian Courses (3+)	87
Require Chapel	87
Christian Reasoning in Student Conduct Code	84
Require Christian Courses (4+)	71
Require Students to Be Christian	50
Require Christian Courses (5+)	50
VP for Mission / Chaplain on Executive Leadership Team	21
Community Covenant	18

Note: N = 38.

Tables 6.4 and 6.5 provide a list of these institutions based on the
key dividing line of student admission policies and whether they admit
non-Christian students. Table 6.4 lists those institutions that do not
require students to be Christian to attend, with almost all scores ranging from 15 to 20.

Table 6.4. Low Church Institutions That Do Not Require Students to Be Christian

Institution Name	Required Christian Courses	VP for Mission	Covenant	OCIG Score
Freed-Hardeman University	3	No	No	15
Pacific Union College	6	No	No	15
Rochester College	3	No	No	15
Andrews University	4	No	No	16
Bluffton University	3	No	No	16
Eastern Mennonite University	3	No	Yes	16
Florida College	2	No	No	16
Southwestern Adventist University	4	Yes	No	16
University of Mobile	2	No	No	16
Belmont University	2	Yes	No	17
Eastern University	2	No	Yes	17
Loma Linda University	4	No	No	17
Bethesda Christian University	6	No	No	18
Grove City College	3	Yes	No	18
La Sierra University	4	No	No	18
Ohio Valley University	6	No	No	18
Liberty University	6	Yes	No	20
Pillar College	7	No	No	20
Arlington Baptist University	10	No	No	24

As can be seen, one major difference among the institutions in Table 6.4 is the number of required Christian courses in each (ranging from two to ten).

Table 6.5 lists those high-scoring Low Church institutions that require all students to be Christian. Their scores range between 16 and 25—a range that is slightly higher than those listed in Table 6.4.

Table 6.5. Low Church Institutions That Require Students to Be Christian

Institution Name	Required Christian Courses	VP for Mission	Covenant	OCIG Score
Kansas Christian College	2	No	No	16
Crowley's Ridge College Arkansas	4	No	No	17
Summit Christian College	2	No	No	17
Southwestern Assemblies of God University	4	No	Yes	18
Baptist College of Florida	4	No	No	19
Truett-McConnell University	5	No	No	19
Baptist University of the Americas	5	No	Yes	20
Randall University	5	No	No	20
Trinity Baptist College	4	Yes	No	20
Bob Jones University	5	Yes	Yes	21
Ecclesia College	8	No	No	22
Calvary University	7	Yes	No	23
The Master's University	7	Yes	Yes	23
Boyce College	9	No	Yes	24
Dallas Christian College	10	No	Yes	25
Great Lakes Christian College	10	No	No	25
Oak Hills Christian College	10	No	No	25
Spurgeon College	10	No	No	25
World Mission University	10	No	No	25

All those institutions scoring 22 or above require seven or more Christian courses. Not surprisingly, most are small institutions that enroll less than four hundred students (Boyce College, Spurgeon College, and the Master's University are the three exceptions).

CONCLUSION

Independent Low Church Protestant colleges and universities are a unique subset of institutions within US Christian higher education.

For the average student or parent exploring Christian colleges and universities, it would be reasonable to expect Protestant institutions to be broadly similar. Although Protestant institutions of all types are likely to share certain doctrinal beliefs, the OCIG helps illuminate the diverse ways the Christian identity guides administrative decisions. Low Church OCIG scores reveal almost opposite patterns in administrative decision-making scores and categories from their mainline Protestant counterparts. And as this chapter reveals, OCIG scores and categories across the sixty-two independent Low Church Protestant institutions evaluated are impressively diverse.

Thus, we urge you—our readers who are interested in Protestant institutions—to evaluate these colleges and universities not just based on their broad historical or denominational affiliations but according to the ways their Christian identity is uniquely operationalized in their administrative decisions. The latter (administrative decisions) are far more determinant of an individual's lived experience on campus than the former (historical affiliations). Thus, we encourage the use of the OCIG to help students, parents, and staff explore the various components of institutional culture most important to them in their decision-making processes.

CHAPTER 7

The One Eastern Orthodox College

One of the unusual characteristics of Eastern Orthodox higher education is how late it started. The Catholic and Orthodox Churches officially split in 1054. Around 150 years later, the oldest existing universities in the world developed in Western Christendom with the support of the Catholic Church.[1] Yet no Orthodox institutions that scholars classify as universities were started for the next 750 years.

Several important social, political, and theological differences help explain the failure of national Eastern Orthodox churches to develop their own universities. First, in the history of the Western Church, popes successfully achieved a greater degree of institutional autonomy and power separate from the state. In contrast, the Eastern Church more often found itself, for both political and theological reasons, serving in a less autonomous and powerful role within the dominant political structure. Consequently, when political entities designed and created institutions of higher education, the Orthodox Church had limited leadership and influence in institutions originally designed and created to serve the interests of the state ahead of the ends of the church.[2]

Second, during the time church-sponsored universities were developing in medieval Europe, many Orthodox lands were ruled or threatened by foreign powers. The Islamic Ottoman Empire controlled the contemporary area around Greece, Bulgaria, Romania, and Serbia; various Catholic rulers often controlled large swaths of Orthodox territory, and Russia lay under Mongol rule.[3] These situations led to a rapid decline in lower forms of Orthodox education.[4]

Third, the educational institutions the Orthodox Church did develop in lands free from foreign domination, such as Russia, were usually seminaries formed primarily for training priests. Some seminaries did offer a much broader curriculum, helping train doctors and jurists. Nonetheless, in comparison to clerical education in the West, Eastern seminaries placed less emphasis on subjects beyond classical languages, theology, and the Church Fathers.

In addition, neither the humanistic revival during the Renaissance nor the education explosion induced by the Reformation would significantly influence most Orthodox lands. As a result, there are no early educational theories proposed by Orthodox thinkers to mirror those found in Catholicism and Protestantism by figures such as Erasmus, Ignatius of Loyola, or John Amos Comenius.

Finally, some features of Orthodox theology itself played a key role in the stunted development of the educational offerings at Orthodox institutions. The historical emphasis of Orthodoxy upon—and its comfort with—mystery, its views of the limitations of reason, and its emphasis upon apophatic theology (theology by negation) did not inspire systematizing and rationalizing in theology.[5] As Daniel Clendenin writes, "In Eastern theologians, we find nothing at all that would compare with Aquinas's *Summa Theologica*, Calvin's *Institutes of the Christian Religion*, or Karl Barth's *Church Dogmatics*. . . . Adoration, contemplation, and vision, not rational intellection, characterize the Eastern tradition."[6] Consequently, Orthodox educational institutions often did not emphasize the importance of developing systematic knowledge in a variety of fields.[7]

Catholic universities are over eight hundred years old, and Protestant universities are over five hundred years old. In contrast, the history of Eastern Orthodox Christian universities can be said to span less than seventy-five years.[8] In the United States, there is only one four-year undergraduate multidisciplinary Eastern Orthodox college (Hellenic College); it started in 1968.[9]

Interestingly, Hellenic College educates less than one hundred undergraduates and primarily appeals to Greek Orthodox students instead of the wide range of Orthodox churches from Russia, Ukraine, Romania, Bulgaria, and so forth. For example, its vision statement says it seeks "to be the intellectual, educational and spiritual formation center of the Greek Orthodox Archdiocese of America, stimulating, developing, and sustaining ordained and lay vocations for service to Church and society, based on faith."[10] It does not even include other Orthodox churches in the United States (e.g., Russian Orthodox) in its vision.

Considering the particular focus of Hellenic College, it is not surprising that it scores high on the Operationalizing Christian Identity Guide (16). The school openly advertises itself as Orthodox, requires the faculty and leadership to be Orthodox, and requires two courses related to the Orthodox tradition, and the Orthodox identity influences both the worship and ethos of the community. Unfortunately, though, the Orthodox Church has not placed its resources into fostering Christian higher education around the world. In most Orthodox countries, it has relied on state institutions to both support Orthodox theological education and support an Orthodox ecclesial monopoly.

CHAPTER 8

Evaluating the Diversity of Christian Higher Education in the United States

A group of higher education scholars once claimed that "every college has two missions"—the *espoused* mission and the *enacted* mission.[1] The former refers to the official campus mission statement, and the latter refers to "what the institution actually does and who it serves."[2] In other words, the espoused mission is what an institution says it does, and the enacted mission is what it puts into practice. The scholars argued that greater alignment between these two missions leads to improved student engagement and "success." This finding is no less true for Christian higher education. And yet, despite a growing body of literature on the unique ways institutions manifest their Christian missions,[3] the larger field of higher education continues to consider Christian higher education as a monolith.[4]

The trend of grouping schools solely based on espoused missions is troublesome in that it obscures the very real differences among the enacted missions of the 546 Christian colleges and universities in the United

States (366 Protestant, 179 Catholic, and 1 Eastern Orthodox) and 16 institutions in Canada (5 Catholic and 11 Protestant). Indeed, if this book has one central argument, it is this: Christian institutions vary considerably in the degree to which they operationalize a Christian identity. We created the Operationalizing Christian Identity Guide (OCIG) to guide readers through the various ways Christian missions are enacted within the field of Christian higher education. Thus far we have made this argument by exploring nuances *within* the six traditions we used to group the colleges and institutions. In this chapter, we will explore the nuances *among* those six traditions. First, we will compare schools by exploring patterns within larger institutional categories, then we will identify the key ways schools enact their Christian missions that contribute to overall OCIG scores.

COMPARING INSTITUTIONAL TYPES

In previous chapters, we divided Protestant institutions into several subcategories and explored nuances within them, but how do all these subcategories compare with one another? To answer this question, we begin our comparisons by looking at similarities and differences among Protestant institutions. Then, we compare the similarities and differences between Catholic and Protestant institutions as a whole. Overall, our findings indicate the two types of institutional groupings that operationalize their Christian identity significantly are CCCU/IACE (Council for Christian Colleges and Universities / International Alliance for Christian Education) institutions and other Low Church Protestant institutions.

GENERAL PROTESTANT PATTERNS

There are two clear patterns of difference among Protestant institutions. Almost every (95 percent) mainline Protestant institution and historically Black college and university (HBCU) score 12 or below, with only eight total exceptions. On the other hand, nearly every CCCU/IACE and Low Church Protestant institution scores 12 or above (93 percent), with fourteen exceptions from the Low Church Protestant category (see Figure 8.1). Thus, if you are looking for Protestant institutions operationalizing their Christian missions in significant ways, you will typically find such institutions among the CCCU/IACE or Low Church Protestant colleges and universities. The reasons for the differences among all four Protestant groups are indicated in Table 8.1.

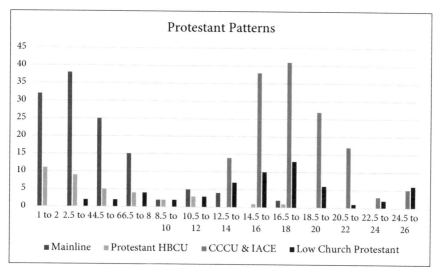

Figure 8.1. Score Ranges for Various Protestant Groupings

Table 8.1. Prevalence of Empirical Markers by Protestant Grouping

Administrative Decision-Making Category	Mainline Protestant Institutions	Protestant HBCUs	CCCU/IACE Institutions	Low Church Protestant Institutions
Voluntary but Privileged Chapel	79%	83%	99%	97%
Require at least Partial Christian Membership for Board	55%	46%	100%	86%
Only Christian Student Groups	44%	63%	91%	89%
"About Us" Page Mentions Christian Identity	36%	51%	100%	77%
Mission Statement Mentions Christian Mission	33%	37%	100%	95%
Require Christian Courses (1+)	31%	29%	100%	87%
Require President to Be Christian	23%	17%	100%	89%
Code of Conduct Mentions Christianity	20%	29%	98%	90%
VP for Mission / Chaplain on Executive Leadership Team	15%	3%	20%	18%
Christian Reasoning or Covenant in Conduct Code	13%	11%	90%	73%
Home Page Mentions Christian Identity	13%	20%	89%	73%
Christian Department	10%	20%	95%	71%
Require Christian Courses (2+)	10%	11%	95%	73%
Require Board to Be Christian	9%	9%	100%	76%
Require Christian Membership for Faculty	6%	9%	98%	76%
Require Christian Membership for Staff	5%	9%	97%	71%
Require Chapel/Mass	4%	34%	87%	66%
Require Christian Courses (3+)	2%	11%	64%	58%
Require Christian Courses (4+)	1%	9%	45%	45%
Christian Centers or Institutes	2%	3%	15%	8%
Require Christian Membership for Students	0%	3%	29%	32%

Note: N = 120 mainline Protestants, 35 Protestant HBCUs, 149 CCCU/IACE, and 62 Low Church Protestants.

INTER/NONDENOMINATIONAL VERSUS DENOMINATIONAL PATTERNS

The nondenominational university is a uniquely US invention. No such thing existed in the rest of the world before its emergence in the early United States. Oberlin College (1833) can be considered the first nondenominational college of this type. Emerging out of the progressive fires of the Second Great Awakening, the support of the founders of Oberlin for abolitionism and other moral crusades—along with the association of the institution with evangelist Charles Grandison Finney—earned the school notoriety. Oberlin was also known for many other noteworthy firsts. For instance, it was the first coeducational institution in the United States and one of the first to admit African Americans.[5] Despite this original evangelical focus, Oberlin secularized rather quickly. The school maintained its radical progressive spirit, but it cast off most aspects of its Christian heritage by the time of World War I.[6]

The history of the secularization of Oberlin was not the norm for nondenominational colleges. Indeed, several nondenominational Christian colleges founded after Oberlin have maintained their Christian identity. Over the past 150 years, three types of nondenominational institutions have emerged. Though some began without any denominational affiliation (e.g., Biola University, John Brown University, and Westmont College), others became inter- or nondenominational through leadership choices or mergers (e.g., Asbury University, Azusa Pacific University, Colorado Christian University, Gordon College, Hillsdale College, Taylor University, and Wheaton College). More recently, individuals associated with particular movements or churches but not specific denominations have founded nondenominational institutions (e.g., Oral Roberts University and Regent University). Overall, this set of institutions gives evidence of a common evangelical tendency throughout US history—the propensity to focus on certain common Christian beliefs about the Bible, Christ, salvation, and activism that cross denominational boundaries and serve as a source for common partnerships.[7]

James Burtchaell, a theologian who studied the secularization of higher education, worried that a set of shared beliefs would be weaker than denominational ties. This hypothesis led him to argue that nondenominational colleges were more prone to secularization. More recent research has challenged Burtchaell's claim, finding minimal significant differences between the secularization of denominational and nondenominational institutions.[8] Our OCIG supports and extends the recent empirical findings by highlighting some of the important nuances between these two types of institutions.

Figure 8.2 helps us understand the differences. All the mainline Protestant and HBCU institutions are denominationally related, so we simply separated the nondenominational institutions that are affiliated with the CCCU and Low Church Protestantism from the denominational CCCU and Low Church institutions. As one can see from the figure, there is little evidence that nondenominational institutions are more likely to secularize. The opposite is true.

There is no indication that nondenominational colleges and universities are less likely to operationalize their Christian identity. For example,

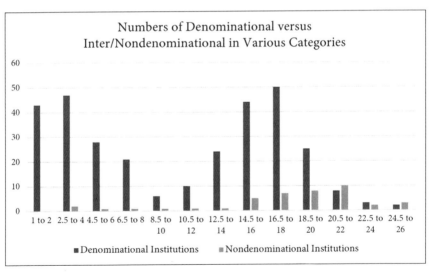

Figure 8.2. Denominational versus Inter/Nondenominational in Various Categories

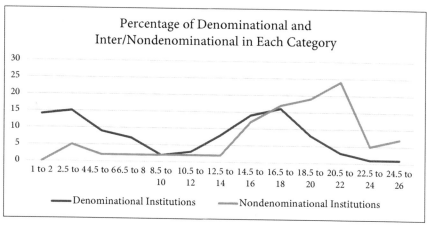

Figure 8.3. Denominational versus Inter/Nondenominational Patterns as a Percentage of Total

Figure 8.3 reveals that when considering the percentage of institutions in various categories when taken as a whole (by the total of denominational or nondenominational), there are more denominational colleges and universities in the lower and middle score levels, but a higher percentage of nondenominational institutions attempt to operationalize their Christian identity at a significant level.

Overall, we find that the evidence does not support Burtchaell's thesis. Nondenominational institutions are actually more committed to operationalizing their Christian identity.

CATHOLIC VERSUS PROTESTANT PATTERNS

We found several fascinating differences between Catholic and Protestant institutions as well. As mentioned in Chapter Four, not one Catholic institution is completely secular according to the OCIG, but eighty-three Protestant institutions score 0 on our 28-point OCIG and are therefore declassified as "faith-based." In other words, the story of Catholic institutions differs from historic mainline Protestant institutions.

Catholic institutions differed significantly from Protestant institutions at either end of the spectrum. Whereas 71 percent of Protestant institutions score either below 7.5 or 17 and above, 84 percent of Catholic institutions score from 7.5 to 17. In other words, the Protestant institutions tend to gather at the ends of the OCIG, whereas Catholic institutions gather toward the middle (see Figure 8.3). Stated simply, our overall findings reveal the mainline Protestant and HBCU institutions score at the low end of the OCIG, the Catholic institutions score in the middle, and the CCCU, IACE, and Low Church Protestant institutions score at the high end.

One of the major reasons for the difference between high-scoring Protestant institutions and Catholic institutions has to do with membership requirements. Very few Catholic institutions require faculty and staff to be Christian. In addition, only one Catholic institution, the Massachusetts Branch of Thomas Aquinas, requires students to be Catholic. In contrast, 18 percent of Protestant institutions admit only Christian students, and just over half require faculty (56 percent) and staff (54 percent) to be Christian (see Table 8.2).

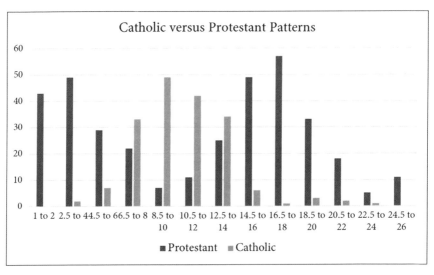

Figure 8.4. Catholic versus Protestant Institutional Scoring in Raw Numbers

Table 8.2. Catholic and Protestant Institutions Receiving Points by Decision-Making Category

Administrative Decision-Making Category	Protestant	Catholic
Voluntary but Privileged Mass/Chapel	90%	100%
Mission Statement Mentions Christian Mission	71%	96%
"About Us" Page Mentions Christian Identity	71%	83%
Require President to Be Christian/Catholic	65%	76%
Only Christian Student Groups	73%	72%
Require Christian Courses (1+)	68%	71%
Christian Department	56%	66%
Christian Centers or Institutes	9%	55%
VP for Mission	17%	55%
Code of Conduct Mentions Christianity	65%	46%
Require Christian Courses (2+)	56%	44%
Require at least Partial Christian Membership for Board	78%	63%
First Web Page Mentions Christian/Catholic Identity	55%	36%
Christian Reasoning or Covenant in Conduct Code	54%	24%
Require Christian Courses (3+)	38%	19%
Require Christian Courses (4+)	27%	8%
Require Christian/Catholic Membership for Faculty	56%	5%
Require Christian/Catholic Membership for Staff	54%	5%
Require Board to Be Christian/Catholic	57%	3%
Require Chapel/Mass	51%	1%
Require Christian Membership for Students	18%	0.6%

Note: N = 179 Catholic, 366 Protestant (120 mainline Protestants, 35 Protestant HBCUs, 149 CCCU/IACE, and 62 Low Church Protestants).

Two other differences highlight a uniquely Catholic pattern. Whereas only 17 percent of Protestant institutions have a vice president for mission and only 9 percent have Christian centers or institutes, 55 percent of Catholic institutions host Christian centers/institutes, and 55 percent have a vice president for mission or priest on the executive leadership team. In these respects, Catholic institutions take a different approach to the intersection of Christianity and administration than Protestant institutions.

IDENTIFYING THE ENACTED MISSION

Having compared the different degrees to which institutions enact their espoused Christian missions, we recognize that not everyone has the time to evaluate a school on all eleven items included in our OCIG. Thus, are there particular elements that signal the tendency of an institution to enact its Christian mission (or not)? We recognize that our eleven-item guide might be cumbersome, so we analyzed the data to see—when standardized—which elements were more closely associated with final OCIG scores. Considering that analysis, these are the top five questions we would encourage our readers to answer as they seek to determine how an institution is enacting its mission.

1. What Mission Does the Institution Espouse on Its Website?

The first step to enacting a mission is often being willing to espouse one. Thus, as you look for an institution that aligns with your approach to Christianity, its website is an easy first place to look to determine how and in what ways the institution is Christian. The fact that an institution espouses its Christian mission on its website does not tell you everything you need to know. Indeed, that is why we felt the need to distinguish between an espoused and enacted mission in the first place, but in general, those who articulate Christian missions on their websites are more likely to have higher total scores than those who do not (see Table 8.3). Schools that mention their Christian missions on either their home pages or "About Us" pages have more than double the OCIG totals. Those who have it on both have more than triple the OCIG score.

Table 8.3. OCIG Total by Website References

Christian Mission	Average OCIG Score	Count
Did Not Mention	4.6	127
Home *or* "About Us" Page Only	9.6	165
Home *and* "About Us" Page	16.1	254

2. With Which Organization(s) Does the School Align?

We found that Christian tradition (Catholic, Protestant, Orthodox) and the orders and denominations within them do not always predict the score of an institution. Schools within these larger categories operationalize their Christian identity in quite distinct ways (as reflected by their OCIG scores). That said, institutions affiliated with the CCCU or the IACE tend to exhibit a certain type of evangelical campus experience. As discussed in Chapter Five, this tendency is largely due to the requirements for membership in these organizations. Conversely, on the Catholic side, institutions aligned with a particular Catholic order have lower OCIG scores. It is the independently lay-led Catholic institutions that have more robustly operationalized their Christian missions. In sum, when looking at an institution, be sure to note its affiliated denomination or order (if it has one)—it can tell you a lot about how the campus enacts its Christian mission.

3. What Courses/Chapel Does the School Require of Students?

Colleges and universities that require students to take courses related to Christianity or require chapel have higher overall OCIG scores. Those who are familiar with academic structures will know just how challenging it can be to change the curriculum—it is not uncommon to take a decade to pass even the slightest of general education reforms. Given how challenging it is to enact curricular change, requiring several courses related to Christianity requires significant support and thus likely reflects a more widespread institutional commitment to the espoused mission (see Table 8.4). On average, schools that require at least one course related to Christianity have more than triple the OCIG total.

Table 8.4. OCIG Total by Course Requirements

Course Requirements	Average OCIG Score	Count
No Courses Required	4.7	168
At Least One Course Required	14.5	378

Requirements related to chapel or mass demonstrate a similar pattern (see Table 8.5). On average, schools that merely privilege Christian chapel/mass have more than double the OCIG score, but institutions that *require* chapel have well over four times the OCIG score.

Table 8.5. OCIG Total by Chapel Requirements

Chapel	Average OCIG Score	Count
No Chapel / Multifaith Chapel	4.1	35
Voluntary but Privileged Chapel/Mass	8.7	320
Require Chapel/Mass	17.5	191

Thus, a glance at what an institution requires of a student academically and regarding chapel/mass attendance is likely to reveal a great deal about how the Christian mission is enacted on that campus.

4. How Does the Institution Justify Its Codes of Conduct?

If the curriculum reveals how the Christian identity of an institution is enacted in the academic space, the code of conduct reveals how the Christian identity is enacted in the cocurricular and social realms of the campus. Thus, it is perhaps unsurprising that we found that the way an institution justifies its code of conduct is tied to its overall OCIG score as well (see Table 8.6).

Table 8.6. OCIG Total by Code of Conduct

Code of Conduct	Average OCIG Score	Count
Legal Language	6.4	226
Broad Moral Language / Christianity Mentioned	11.2	79
Christian Reasoning / Christian Covenant	16.4	241

Institutions that only use legal language in their code of conduct have an average OCIG score of 6.4. Schools that use broadly moral language throughout or reference Christianity in the introduction to their code of conduct score right around the population average (11.2 compared to the population average of 11.5). When schools have a separate community covenant or pledge justified by theological language, however, on average their OCIG score jumps up significantly to 16.4. Our research suggests that one can find a more comprehensive Christian environment in institutions that justify and codify their community life through a code of conduct or community covenant.

5. What Are the Membership Requirements?

An embodiment of the Christian mission requires some person to enact it on campus. Thus, it makes sense that the requirements for students, faculty, staff, presidents, and governing boards to be Christian would have an impact on the operationalization of the Christian mission (see Table 8.7). On average, institutions with Christian identity requirements for any of these positions have well over double the total OCIG score.

Table 8.7. OCIG Total by Membership Requirements

Category	Requirements	Average OCIG Score	Count
Students			
	No or Partial Requirement	10.2	482
	Christian Identity Requirement	20.8	64
Faculty			
	No or Partial Requirement	7.5	333
	Christian Identity Requirement	17.8	213
Staff			
	No or Partial Requirement	7.6	339
	Christian Identity Requirement	17.8	207
President			
	No or Partial Requirement	5.1	172
	Christian Identity Requirement	14.4	374
Governing Board			
	No or Partial Requirement	7.6	330
	Christian Identity Requirement	17.4	216

Partial requirements would include a requirement that a certain percentage of students, faculty, staff, or board members have a Christian faith or come from a particular denominational background (if Protestant). Partial requirements for the president refer to institutions where it is not an official requirement to be Christian but has—in history—proven to be true of all the presidents.

We found that the membership requirements of an institution likely reflect its commitments in other decisions as well. A good place to look to find these requirements is on the admissions page (for students) and the employment page (for faculty/staff).

CONCLUSION

The tremendous diversity of Christian higher education in the United States is exemplified both within and across denominations and traditions, nondenominational institutions included. Though such diversity affords those exploring Christian higher education the freedom to choose from a wide range of institutions, we also acknowledge the difficulty of choosing an institution that is aligned with one's educational goals and priorities. Thus, in this chapter, we have tried to clarify how institutions in broad denominational or group categories differ from one another in the extent to which they operationalize their Christian identity.

Highlighting these differences can help students, staff, or faculty looking for a specific type of institution. For instance, students who care deeply about being in a Christian community with like-minded student peers and faculty may be surprised to find this desire better fulfilled within a high-scoring nondenominational institution that—despite lacking a singular denominational affiliation—is more likely to admit and hire only Christians. Prospective students are less likely to find such a community at a Catholic university that—though tied more firmly to a faith tradition—may admit a wide range of students from a variety of faith backgrounds. Of course, this is not to say there are no exceptions to our categorizations or that a deeply committed Catholic student would feel more comfortable at a nondenominational institution. A student may find belonging at a CCCU school or Low Church campus, but they could also use the OCIG markers to find an institution that affords them ample opportunities to engage religiously diverse peers and still feel at home when attending a distinctly Catholic mass.

As demonstrated in these examples, we hope that the OCIG will become a tool to help faculty, staff, and students recognize and navigate the complexity of what we have found to be a diverse set of Christian colleges and universities in the United States.

CHAPTER 9

A New Vision for US Christian Higher Education

Centers for Christian Thought

With Karen Melton and Andrew Hansen

A recent study found that nearly 60 percent of US freshmen who identified as Christian (both Protestant and Catholic) chose to attend public or nonsectarian colleges or universities.[1] Such a decision might have once meant foregoing a distinctly Christian approach to higher education, but the rise and growth of a new type of "center"—independent of but adjacent to pluralistic institutions—means that these students can now find a Christian education whether they attend a Christian college or not.

In fact, two decades before George Marsden penned the story of the secularization of the United States' elite mainline Protestant educational institutions, a group of Christians had already begun a unique movement to revitalize Christian education at these now secular institutions.[2] In the ensuing decades, this movement of para-academic centers has continued to grow in size and scope. Protestant and ecumenical versions of these centers often refer to themselves as Christian study centers, whereas Catholic versions of these centers may refer to themselves as institutes for Catholic thought. We will refer to these centers/institutes collectively and ecumenically as "centers for Christian thought" (CCT). Unlike traditional academic centers and institutes directly affiliated with a particular institution and focused on research, CCT are independently funded and are more focused on the intellectual formation of students and faculty at their nearby institution. At present, there are at least forty-two CCT in the United States, and there are plans to establish several new centers and institutes in the coming years.

Despite their decades-long commitment to Christian education next to the campuses of numerous significant US institutions, these CCT often go unmentioned in conversations about Christian higher education.[3] We wanted to include them in this guide for three reasons:

- These centers operationalize a Christian educational identity in many of the same ways that Christian colleges and universities do. All of them have Christian *educational* (and not just evangelistic) missions, use explicit Christian rhetoric, require Christian membership of board members and leaders, have curricular Christian components, and cultivate worship. Some also offer Christian residential housing with similar types of community covenants as other Christian campuses.

- We wanted to make sure that Christian faculty and administrators working on several secular campuses were aware of the resources these centers could provide to them.

- We wanted to encourage administrators and faculty at Christian colleges and universities to see CCT as potential partners rather than as potential competitors in the struggle to meet enrollment goals.

We believe the larger conversation related to faith integration and the perpetuation of the Christian intellectual tradition would benefit from increased dialogue between Christian higher education administrators and CCT leaders. For example, we imagine that Christian faculty or institutions could see these centers as potential partners where explicitly Christian classes and talks could be hosted (perhaps even for credit). They offer a unique opportunity for expanding Christian higher education.

A BRIEF HISTORY OF THE CCT MOVEMENT

The first centers appeared on university campuses in the 1970s. Similar to other parachurch campus ministries like CRU, InterVarsity, or Catholic Newman Centers, the centers operated within the extracurricular (yet unaffiliated) spaces of the secular state and private universities. Yet in a way that's different from these other Christian ministries, the CCT specifically sought to reengage Christian faith and traditions with the *intellectual* life and work of students and faculty within these universities in embodied ways that mirrored the secular university. Thus, although they offered Christian community like other groups, they also held "lectures and seminars that engage[d] topics and themes directly relating Christianity to the academic work of the University" and sought "physical space on or near campus that serve[d] as a place for hospitality."[4] These elements were usually not a key part of other parachurch ministries. Furthermore, Christian faculty at the state and private secular universities often played pivotal roles in the founding and leadership of CCT.[5]

This emphasis on helping students approach the intellectual questions they are encountering in the classroom from the Christian intellectual tradition marks CCT as a unique presence in the pluralistic university. Whereas many Christian organizations (e.g., campus ministries, churches, and Christian student groups) tend to concentrate on the spiritual, devotional, and social lives of students, CCT are distinct in their effort to complement and transform the intellectual mission of the university.

Table 9.1. A List of CCT Serving State and Private Secular Universities

Member Centers of the Consortium of Christian Study Centers	
Name	Affiliated University / Location
Alcuin Study Center	Ball State University (Muncie, IN)
Anselm House	University of Minnesota (Minneapolis, MN)
Arizona Center for Christian Studies	Arizona State University (Phoenix, AZ)
Augustine Center	Georgetown University (Washington, DC)
Biblical Studies Center	Boise State University (Boise, MT)
Bradley Study Center	Virginia Tech (Blacksburg, VA)
Center for Christian Study	University of Virginia (Charlottesville, VA)
Center for Christianity and Scholarship	Duke University (Durham, NC)
Chesterton House	Cornell University (Ithaca, NY)
Christian Study Center of Champaign–Urbana	University of Illinois (Champaign, IL)
Christian Study Center of Chattanooga	University of Tennessee (Chattanooga, TN)
Christian Study Center of Gainesville	University of Florida (Gainesville, FL)
Cogito	Hampden Sydney College (VA)
Comenius Institute	Indiana University, Purdue University (IN)
C. S. Lewis Study Center	Five Colleges of Massachusetts
Eleazar Wheelock Society	Dartmouth College (Hanover, NH)
Hill House	University of Texas (Austin, TX)
Humanitas Forum on Christianity and Culture	Tennessee Tech University (Cookeville, TN)
Joseph & Alice McKeen Study Center	Bowdoin College (Brunswick, ME)
Mere Christianity Forum	Furman University (Greensville, SC)
New College Berkeley	University of California (Berkeley, CA)

Member Centers of the Consortium of Christian Study Centers	
Name	Affiliated University / Location
North Carolina Study Center	University of North Carolina (Chapel Hill, NC)
The Octet Collaborative	Massachusetts Institute of Technology (MA)
Oread Center	University of Kansas (Lawrence, KS)
Richmond Center for Christian Study	University of Richmond (Richmond, VA)
Rivendell Institute	Yale University (New Haven, CT)
Saint Thomas Mission	University of British Columbia (Vancouver, BC)
Scholé House	Virginia Commonwealth University (Richmond, VA)
Theological Horizons	University of Virginia (Charlottesville, VA)
Trinity Fellowship	Indiana University (Bloomington, IN)
Upper House	University of Wisconsin (Madison, WI)
Via Christian Study Center	Christopher Newport University (Yorktown, VA)
Additional Centers Not Affiliated with the Consortium of Christian Study Centers	
Name	Affiliated University / Location
Aquinas Institute for Catholic Thought	University of Colorado (Boulder, CO)
Beatrice Institute	University of Pittsburgh / Carnegie Mellon University (PA)
Collegium Institute	University of Pennsylvania (Philadelphia, PA)
IKON Institute	Tulane University (New Orleans, LA)
Institute for Faith and Culture	University of Kansas (Lawrence, KS)
Lumen Christi Institute	University of Chicago (Chicago, IL)
Newman Institute for Catholic Thought & Culture	University of Nebraska (Lincoln, NE)
Nova Forum for Catholic Thought	University of Southern California (Los Angeles, CA)
St. Anselm Institute for Catholic Thought	University of Virginia (Charlottesville, VA)

OPERATIONALIZING CHRISTIAN MISSIONS IN THE CCT MOVEMENT

To date, no uniform CCT model exists. The shaping of these institutions occurs at the local level, and only with the establishment of the Consortium of Christian Study Centers (CCSC) in 2009 have some of these institutions sought closer collaboration with one another. This network now convenes and resources more than thirty CCSC member institutions across the United States (see Table 9.1). Despite the diversity of programmatic offerings among the study centers, the CCSC identifies a common mission among its members as the "integration of faith and learning with life" and the "nurturing of Christian faith in the context of the contemporary university."[6] At a recent gathering of study center leaders, Karl Johnson, the current executive director of the CCSC, suggested that the founding of CCT was the very natural human response to the increasing fragmentation of knowledge and the universities that cultivate it. Thus, CCT operationalize their Christian missions by addressing the human inclination to pursue "the integrated life." This approach motivates all their decisions, including the creation of avenues that help overcome fragmentation, particularly the separation of faith and intellect on college campuses.

Vision: For the Good of the University

If the shared motivation and mission of the centers and institutes are the integrated and holistic Christian life for individuals, the long-term future they envision (as a result of achieving their mission) is a healthier university and a healthier church. That is, by equipping and educating students and faculty with the riches of the Christian intellectual tradition, CCT promote the good of the church, which then enhances the university through the "faithful presence" of more integrated Christians.[7] This vision for a healthy university is why leaders typically describe CCT as "para-academic" organizations.

Content: The Riches of the Christian Intellectual Tradition

Although CCT are not accredited academic institutions, they nonetheless offer academic experiences in the extracurricular space of the university. Perhaps unsurprisingly, their curricular decisions are significantly influenced by their Christian missions and their goal of helping students and faculty pursue an integrated life and further the good of the university. According to the CCT we have studied, the curriculum that leads to these ends is a robust exploration of "the riches of the Christian intellectual tradition." Although the exact content depends on the particular center—and the particular program within that center—in general, students and faculty engage in a range of texts intended to expose them to foundational questions (e.g., What does it mean to be human? How do you reconcile faith and science? Can we trust the Bible?) and explore how Christians have answered those questions throughout history.

Some centers provide direct theological education. For example, one center invites first-year students to study the story of redemptive history in the Bible over the course of an academic year—the Old Testament in the fall and the New Testament in the spring. In addition to Scripture (and Tradition for Catholic institutes), others engage—through reading groups, lectures, and seminars—the writings of Plato, Aristotle, Augustine, Aquinas, and Calvin, as well as more modern writers who engage them (e.g., John Henry Newman, Alasdair MacIntyre, and James K. A. Smith). Still others explore how Christian theology (including Catholic social teaching for some) informs—or ought to inform—various disciplines like criminal justice, economics, or medicine. The curricula of CCT tend to emphasize the humanities as a helpful corrective to the increasingly pragmatic approaches of contemporary higher education. The philosophical inquiry and reflection, they argue, are what ought to motivate and guide the pursuit of practical knowledge in the first place.

These riches of the Christian tradition, whether conveyed through multiyear fellows programs or a collection of one-off lectures (both of which were offered at every CCT), form what amounts to a supplemental core curriculum that provides a model of Christian intellectualism for faculty and students to follow. The programs help students and faculty "think Christianly" and apply theological thinking to all of life.[8]

Methods: Hospitality and Intellectual Fellowship

How do CCT help students and faculty pursue an integrated life for the good of the university? In short, through hospitality that leads to intellectual fellowship. CCT open their space (often an office on campus or a house adjacent to campus) to students and faculty for intellectual fellowship over food, coffee, and tea—sometimes in conjunction with a lecture or discussion group, other times just a space to study or work. CCT leaders view hospitality as a significant and primary way of connecting with students and faculty and inviting them into the riches of the Christian intellectual tradition. Hospitality is central because it is the means of cultivating a particular kind of intellectual fellowship. As one of the CCT leaders said, "I think there's an assumption baked into our organization that the kind of education and spiritual transformation we're seeking happens primarily through relationship—with God and others." Students and faculty form a unique bond with the CCT staff and one another as they share regular meals and think deeply together. In this way, hospitality is a method to attract—but also to transform—those with whom the CCT interact.

In sum, CCT use hospitality and intellectual fellowship to create a thick moral community dedicated to satiating the human appetite to live an integrated life.[9] The practitioners leading these centers firmly believe that living an integrated life will also have societal-level effects—equipping the global church and thereby benefiting the university and society. By equipping students and faculty to engage their callings to the intellectual life in the context of the Christian narrative, CCT help the university to be what it was meant to be: a beacon of coherent truth for all of society.

OPPORTUNITIES FOR MUTUAL LEARNING

Despite the distinctions we have made between Christian colleges and CCT, the two could benefit from increased dialogue and resource sharing. Both are seeking to cultivate the Christian life of the mind and have cultivated wisdom from decades (and centuries) of attempting to do so. For example, the Christian college commitment to "integrate biblical truth . . . throughout the academic enterprise"[10] has led to significant developments in the faith and learning conversation, including what it means for research, teaching, graduate education, and specific disciplinary applications.[11] New learning in these areas is communicated nearly daily on the *Faith Animating Learning* blog (https://christianscholars.com/blog) hosted by *Christian Scholar's Review*. CCT leaders who are responsible for engaging faculty on their pluralistic campuses could benefit greatly from these resources.

Likewise, faculty from Christian colleges and universities could benefit from hearing about the Christian education happening at CCT on pluralistic campuses. The flexibility and entrepreneurial spirit of the CCT could help expose areas in which Christian higher education has—perhaps unwittingly—continued to rely on standards and structures merely because "that's the way it has always been done." For example, the use of hospitality to promote intellectual fellowship in CCT serves as a helpful reminder of the value of organic and smaller-scale offerings.

Finding ways for mutual learning and dialogue between CCT and Christian higher education could also help further the joint purpose of perpetuating the Christian intellectual tradition. For example, one of us (Perry) recently noted how the faith and learning conversation in Christian higher education can sometimes become insular and overly critical—the perspective provided by CCT staff on pluralistic campuses could help maintain a more balanced approach to critique and creativity.[12] Additionally, although we hope many Christian graduate students associated with CCT would continue to seek employment in pluralistic settings, establishing connections with Christian colleges during graduate school could help identify and train future Christian college faculty as well. If future faculty engaged with CCT during graduate school, it could alleviate some of the strain felt by Christian institutions trying to develop faculty for Christian mission after they are hired.[13]

CONCLUSION

In his article introducing the CCT movement, Andrew Hansen suggests Christian study centers (in particular) operate like a "Christian college in a food truck."[14] The food truck metaphor implies that centers share the same mission as Christian colleges but with limited or reimagined offerings. In many ways, this analogy is apt—CCT use hospitality and intellectual fellowship as a means of fostering Christian education in a manner that is quite similar to the way residential communities form students on Christian college campuses. Students are mentored and trained by CCT staff in ways that are similar to how students at Christian colleges receive mentorship from student development staff or intellectual fellowship through core curricula.[15] And yet, despite the similarities, we believe the CCT mission articulates something that Christian colleges often merely assume—the need to integrate identity pieces into a cohesive whole.

The reality is that Christian colleges and universities (just like all colleges and universities) are often bound to and formed by external forces such as accrediting bodies and societal assumptions about what a college is supposed to be.[16] As a result, Christian colleges and universities do an excellent job developing a range of identities through programs in a variety of different departments but, as a result of their structures, can struggle at times to help students see how the Christian faith guides the pieces so that they fit together into a single whole.[17]

In contrast to this fragmented approach, CCT staff seem to embody a reality one of us (Perry) has argued for in the past—namely, how the Christian intellectual tradition "provides us the wisdom and the guidance needed to pursue wholeness and excellence without idolatry."[18] Indeed, it seems to us that the mission and motivation to pursue wholeness for the sake of the university is the central animating principle of the CCT. Thus, we would describe CCT as a place to help Christian students reimagine the "soul" of the university as they navigate the otherwise "ghostly . . . criterionless" nature of pluralistic campuses.[19] CCT help students and faculty find this soul and thereby equip them to pursue education and research that is animated by Christian faith, even on secular campuses.

CHAPTER 10

Canadian Christian Colleges and Universities

To understand the size and scope of Canadian versus US Christian higher education, it helps to know the *total* number of students attending a Catholic or Protestant college, university college, or university in Canada. Combined, their enrollment for 2021 was approximately 18,160—a number that is less than the third-largest Christian university in the United States (Baylor University). Why does a country with 11 percent of the population of the United States only have 1 percent of the total number of students attending Christian institutions of higher education?

There are two important reasons to consider. Part of the explanation relates to the lower church attendance rates among the population. Only 16 percent of Canadians reported attending church at least once a week in 2019, whereas 29 percent of Americans in 2020 had attended church in the last seven days.[1] Still, the more important factor has to do with the history and structure of the system of higher education of each country. As mentioned earlier, up until 1952, the majority of US college students attended private institutions, most of which were Christian.[2] In contrast, in Canada, the dominant churches and the government partnered to form the early institutions of higher education (the Catholic Church in French Canada and the Protestant churches in English Canada).[3] As a result, few private universities, as they are defined in the US context, existed.

Christianity did influence the administration, curriculum, and cocurricular life of early Canadian institutions. Yet in the 1900s, as secularization occurred within the education system of Canada, all early Protestant and most early Catholic universities secularized.[4] Thus, Harry Fernhout notes that "when the process of secularization pervaded Canadian universities in the latter half of the twentieth century, there were virtually no Christian institutions other than Bible colleges and seminaries to provide an alternative to the dominant paradigm."[5]

Today, unlike the United States, the only Protestant institutions remaining are newer, mostly Low Church institutions. As a result, contemporary Canadian Christian higher education is quite young. Only two of the five Catholic universities on our list of Christian colleges or universities in Canada started before 1910. Likewise, the youngest of the eleven Protestant institutions started in 1919 as a Bible college, and most of the remaining eleven only became universities or liberal arts colleges within the last three decades. Thus, although Canada has a long history of higher education, its history of contemporary Christian institutions is rather short.

CURRENT STATUS

Since no older, partially secularized Protestant institutions exist in Canada, the Catholic and Protestant institutions are not spread across the spectrum of our Operationalizing Christian Identity Guide (OCIG) as they are in the United States. Instead, the Catholic institutions are grouped at the lower end—between 5.5 and 10.5—and the Protestant institutions all score between 13 and 25 (see Table 10.1).

Table 10.1. Christian Colleges and Universities in Canada

Institution Name	Church Tradition/ Denomination	Origin Year	Enrollment	OCIG Score
Saint Mary's University	Catholic	1986	600	5.5
Saint Thomas University	Catholic	1910	2,024	5.5
Saint Jerome's University	Catholic	1865	1,019	6.5
Saint Paul University	Catholic	1848	706	7
King's University College	Catholic	1954	3,400	10.5
Burman University	Seventh-day Adventist	1919	479	13
Booth University College	The Salvation Army	1982	322	15
Crandall University	Baptist	1949	1,104	15
Redeemer University	Nondenominational	1982	810	16
The King's University	Interdenominational	1979	910	16
Ambrose University	Nazarene & Alliance	1921	920	18
Providence University College	Evangelical/ Nondenominational	1925	325	18
Tyndale University	Evangelical/ Nondenominational	2003	1,321	18
Trinity Western University	Evangelical Free Church	1962	3,810	19
Canadian Mennonite University	Mennonite	1998	690	20
Briercrest College	Transdenominational	1935	640	25

COMPARISONS TO THE UNITED STATES

Four of the five Catholic institutions in Canada score lower than 89 percent of the US Catholic institutions. The primary differences in Canadian Catholic institutions pertain to rhetoric and course requirements.

Only one of the Canadian institutions, King's University College, is clear about its Catholic identity on its first web page and "About Us" site. King's is also the only one with a vice president for mission—a leadership position held on 55 percent of US Catholic campuses. Finally, only one of the Canadian Catholic institutions requires a course that directly seeks to educate students about Christianity (St. Mary's University), and only two briefly mention Catholicism or Christianity in their student conduct codes (Saint Jerome's University and King's University College). In general, Catholic universities in Canada do not extensively operationalize their Catholic identity to distinguish their institutions from secular universities (see Table 10.2).

Table 10.2. Summary of Catholic Institutions Receiving Points by Decision-Making Category

Administrative Decision-Making Category	Canada (%)	United States (%)
Mission Statement Mentions Catholic Mission	80	96
"About Us" Page Mentions Catholic Identity	60	83
Home Page Mentions Catholic Identity	40	36
Christian Centers or Institutes	40	55
Require Christian Courses (1+)	20	71
Christian Department	20	66
VP for Mission / Chaplain on Executive Leadership Team	20	55
Code of Conduct Mentions Catholicism	20	46
Require Christian Courses (2+)	0	44
Christian Covenant or Christian Reasoning in Conduct Code	0	24

Note: N = 5 for Canada and 179 for the United States.

In contrast to the Catholic institutions in Canada, Protestant institutions are more thoroughly Christian in membership and their curricular and cocurricular decisions. All the Protestant institutions in Canada are similar to the top half of Protestant institutions in the United States. In general, the Protestant institutions in Canada score close to the US-based Council for Christian Colleges and Universities (CCCU) institutions (all CCCU member types); indeed, eight of the eleven are members of the CCCU. All but one have a clear Christian mission, and all have the same Christian membership requirements for faculty, staff, and leadership (while not having any for students). Moreover, all have only Christian student religious groups on their campuses.

The major difference among Protestant institutions in Canada has to do with the number of required Bible, theology, or Christian courses (ranging from one to ten). A few other minor differences related to the name of the department addressing Christianity in the curriculum, the space given to Christian reasoning in the cocurricular codes of conduct, the existence of Christian centers or institutes, and whether chapel is voluntary or mandated (see Table 10.3).

Table 10.3. Summary of Institutions Receiving Points by Decision-Making Category

Administrative Decision-Making Category	Canadian	CCCU (US-based)
Mission Statement Mentions Christian Mission	91%	100%
Require Board & President to Be Christian	100%	100%
Require Christian Courses (1+)	100%	100%
"About Us" Page Mentions Christian Identity	100%	100%
Require All Faculty to be Christian	100%	98%
Only Christian Student Groups	100%	90%
Require Christian Courses (2+)	91%	95%
Home Page Mentions Christian Identity	81%	90%
Christian Department	72%	94%
Require Chapel	72%	87%
Require Christian Courses (3+)	72%	66%
Christian Centers or Institutes	72%	17%
Christian Reasoning in Covenant or Conduct Code	63%	90%

Table 10.3. Summary of Institutions Receiving Points by Decision-Making Category (*continued*)

Administrative Decision-Making Category	Canadian	CCCU (US-based)
Require Christian Courses (4+)	36%	45%
VP for Mission / Chaplain on Executive Leadership Team	18%	20%
Christian Covenant for Resident Halls	9%	25%
Require Christian Membership for Students	0%	27%

Note: $N = 11$ for Canadian institutions and 134 for US institutions.

CONCLUSION

Overall, based on the number of students and OCIG scores, the future of Christian higher education in Canada will likely be limited in scale and divided into two clear approaches. We predict Catholics will take what we described in the Catholic chapter as the basic Catholic university approach. They will have a Catholic mission, favored mass, and a strong Catholic cocurricular presence, but the curricular portion of the university will not demonstrate evidence of the Catholic identity, and the membership requirements will only be for the president.

In contrast, we suspect that Protestant higher education in Canada will continue to be Low Church and function like the evangelical or nondenominational approaches present in the United States. Mainline Protestant higher education in Canada has died.

CONCLUSION

Using the Results of Our Guide

Messages for Parents, Students, Faculty,
Staff, Administrators, and Boards

T he way to learn what an institution truly loves is to look at its goals, its rationale for meeting those goals, the policies and incentive systems created to reach those goals, and the account-ability structures for reporting results. The purpose of this book is to take a clear-eyed empirical view of those policies. We believe parents, students, faculty, and staff need this kind of information as they make institutional decisions. They need tools by which they can better dis-cern the relationship between the Christian identity and administrative policies. In this final chapter, we want to provide specific messages to different groups about how best to use this guide.

ADVICE FOR PARENTS, STUDENTS, FACULTY, AND STAFF

One of the glories of North American higher education is the vast diver-sity that exists in both the United States and Canada. Thus, in their search for certain kinds of universities, parents, students, faculty, and staff first need to figure out what kind of university they want for their children or themselves. One can find the most variety in the world in North America. There are secular universities with centers for Christian thought and private Protestant, Catholic, Eastern Orthodox, and nondenominational universities with a vast range of ways of operationalizing their Christian identity. Of course, there are also universities with Christian-sounding names that have secularized (e.g., Texas Christian University and Southern Methodist University).

In this guide, we intentionally compiled and categorically presented previously unprocessed data to help readers make informed decisions within the higher education landscape. First, we sought to make sure that readers are not confused between formerly Christian institutions such as Wake Forest University or Furman University and those institutions that still operationalize some aspect of their Christian missions.

Second, we revealed the various means by which institutions operationalize a Christian identity. In that way, you can discern the institution that best fits your interests. For example, if you want an institution that provides some basic favoritism toward Christian worship on campus but you are not interested in attending chapel or taking courses that will educate you about Christianity, then you should attend a mainline Protestant institution. In contrast, if you want to attend an institution that operationalizes its Christian identity throughout the university in areas of membership requirements, curriculum, and cocurriculum, you should look to institutions with high Operationalizing Christian Identity Guide (OCIG) scores that can be found among certain Catholic and evangelical institutions. Of course, there are also a wide variety of Catholic and Protestant institutions that land somewhere in between those two types.

Many of the administrative markers identified by the OCIG presumably have a direct impact on the lived experiences on campus. Thus, the guide appeals to the interests and priorities of these individuals, but we know that parents are perhaps often key influencers in the decision-making processes of their students and likely constitute a significant portion of our readership. Thus, we hope this guide affords parents comparable levels of insight by which to advise and support the college search of the young adults under their care.

A FINAL MESSAGE FOR BOARDS
AND ADMINISTRATORS

Beyond guiding parents, students, faculty, and staff, we also want to speak to the major group in charge of making changes to many of these policies that indicate an operationalization of the Christian identity of their institution—board members and senior administrators at Christian universities. First, we hope that this guide can help make them aware of their current policies and the policies of related institutions. Second, we think it will provide them with insight into how other institutions undertake these endeavors in case they want to change how they operationalize their Christian missions. Some may want to strengthen their efforts, while others may want to move toward greater secularization so that they imitate prestigious secularized private universities.

Regarding the latter group, we do not think we need to offer much in the way of specific advice because our guide presents a fairly comprehensive overview of the various decisions that lead to a more secularized campus experience. Our only encouragement would be for institutional administrators to be transparent about how they hope to embody their Christian missions. A great model to follow is one we saw on several websites. Some schools had a robust section on their "About Us" pages outlining their historical affiliation with—and present distance from—their founding denomination or Christian tradition. Then toward the end of that section, the schools clearly outlined how that historic connection was or was not manifest in the current campus experience. Most often, we saw schools clarify their distance from Christianity before describing how they retained the spirit of "tolerance," "service," "kindness," or other pluralistic virtues that flowed from their historic connection to faith.

Regarding the former group—those interested in enacting their Christian missions more widely—we will offer some more specific guidance. After all, institutional leaders often receive little formal, or even informal, education about how to create policies and systems that incentivize and reward actions that further the Christian mission of a university. Perhaps they have expertise regarding some of the basic parts of the university (e.g., financial, legal, and basic administrative responsibility), but they may not understand how to advance a distinctly Christian educational mission.

Now, we want to be clear: basic competence in administering financial, legal, and other areas is fundamental to subsequently fulfilling a Christian mission. Competent functional administration is an important indicator of leadership credibility. A student affairs professional once described the problem to us in this way: "So, if a student comes to you and says, 'My toilet is broken,' and you never get it fixed, then when you want to say, 'Let me speak into your life spiritually,' they're going to go, 'You don't care about me.' So, we've got to show that we care and can do our jobs effectively and efficiently, first."[1] Taking care of the budget, avoiding human resources or Title IX mistakes, and ensuring justice in hiring, pay, and so on *are* essential parts of the Christian mission. Yet professional excellence alone does not make an institution *Christian*.

If institutional leaders wish to increase the operationalization of their Christian identity and the missions of their institutions, they could go about changing some of the policies we measured in the OCIG in ways that take into account Christian identity more robustly. Yet we want to caution board members or administrative leaders about simply changing these policies. The elements we identified in our guide are best understood as the *fruit* of a particular type of institutional culture.

We contend that the most important changes to promote the Christian mission among faculty and staff should only come after developing a more robust vision for what we call Christ-animating administration. Only by developing this robust vision will changes to operationalize the Christian mission succeed. To understand this vision, we think it is helpful to describe the differences among Christ-assumed, Christ-added, and Christ-animating administration.

Settling for Christ-Assumed or
Christ-Added Administration

We think it would be interesting for educational leaders to try an experiment during an academic year. Gather recordings of all Christian administrators' start-of-the-year speeches. Then, cut the first five to ten minutes (the prayer and obligatory comments about the mission). After cutting those five to ten minutes, could a person tell the institutional context from the remaining fifty minutes?

We suspect that at many institutions, the institutional context would not be overtly apparent. In other words, our guess is most Christian administrators practice what we call a Christ-assumed or Christ-added approach to administration.[2] They acknowledge the Christian mission, but when it comes to talking about recruitment, admissions, retention, the budget, five-year graduation rates, and various other administrative concerns, administrators at Christian institutions effectively function and speak like secular administrators. Certainly, this kind of thinking is apparent in our empirical findings.

Administrators often overlook more advanced accountability regarding the Christian development of faculty, staff, and students because they do not know how to articulate and theologically defend specific Christian ends, let alone reach those ends. Plus, their efforts in this area are hard to measure (although our OCIG scale is meant to address that problem). Therefore, board members and senior administrators tend to focus on more measurable goals. They get excited about new buildings, new projects, giving, faculty members and students making the news, the new strategic plan (which tends to have vague Christian language but no accountability mechanisms), and the latest athletic success. In our years studying faith integration in Christian higher education, we find that administrators often have clear metrics for meeting strategic goals regarding student enrollment, retention, five-year graduation rates, the budget, building projects, and hiring, which they display at yearly faculty meetings. Yet how they conceptualize, justify, and assess these goals in general or even the means used to accomplish those goals are not always placed in the context of the Christian story—what we call the Christ-animating approach. Does God have anything to do with recruitment, admissions, retention, the budget, five-year graduation rates, and the rest of the administrators' concerns?

For administrators living within a secular story with a focus on power, money, and numbers, the answer would be no. If the rich secular institutions are getting richer, bigger, and more powerful, why would we risk confusing things by trying to add the Christian story into the mix? Indeed, top pluralistic universities are often doing better with retention, budget, five-year graduation rates, and other benchmarks of concern. As a result, Christian administrators often choose peer and aspirant institutions from among these pluralistic institutions and learn "how to do things better" from them.[3] There is certainly a lot that could be learned from these schools, but when we adopt their methods without evaluating their theological presuppositions, we risk subverting our distinctly Christian missions. What is more, when such a practice becomes commonplace, even young Christian faculty and staff who were attracted by and committed to the Christian mission will pick up on the tendency to neglect or minimize it and soon adjust their behavior accordingly.

This problem stems from a dichotomy that emerges when taking a Christ-added approach to administration.[4] Christian administrators detail the well-being of the institution using the general metrics mentioned earlier instead of the well-being of the people within the institution. They think only of the institution and not the people within it. Thus, administrators do not report the overall flourishing of those within the institution: other administrators, faculty, staff, and students.[5] What can administrators do to change? We conclude by offering broad suggestions for administrators to consider.

Christ-Animating versus Christ-Added Christian Administration: Goals

The major difference between Christ-added and Christ-animating administration is that Christ-added administrators merely add a Christian goal to a list of other goals that one would find at a secular university.

In contrast, Christ-animating administrators place all the goals for an institution within the context of the Christian story.

We will use our institution as an example of both approaches. Over the past half decade—relatively recently—the Baylor administration set forth a goal and now recently celebrated reaching R1 status.[6] Some faculty did not like this goal, but we strongly supported it. We desperately needed more Christ-animating scholarship. Yet we observed an initial problem in how the administration approached the goal.

In the beginning, the administration did not repeatedly set forth a clear theological rationale for why they were pursuing R1. Thus, some faculty perceived administrators' desires to reach this goal as motivated purely by a thirst for prestige. Granted, offering theological justifications for administrative goals can be used and abused. Some authoritarian Christian administrators like to play the "God card" and imply that if you do not agree with their goals, then you are not in tune with God, following God, or "all in." But the possible abuse of such an approach—arguments for which are typically rudimentary, based in isolated and reductionistic theology—does not mean we should ask administrators to give up trying to use theological language to place one's goals within the context of the Christian story. Indeed, a robust, positive theological vision that is clearly communicated and cohesively enacted is particularly compelling for a Christian university hoping to operationalize its Christian mission.

Such a theological exercise is vitally important for both administrators and the rest of the educational community. Administrators should be the first to model theological thinking to the faculty at such institutions. Even if an administrator's theological reasoning is faulty at points, at least the ensuing conversation with faculty and staff—if the administration is humble enough to have that conversation—would be a theological one. Moreover, administrators looking to operationalize their Christian missions should want to motivate their faculty and staff by placing one's endeavors within God's cosmic story. By neglecting a Christ-animating approach to goals, administrators risk secularizing their institutions by rationalizing their decisions and motivating faculty and staff in ways mirroring pluralistic institutions.

To their credit, Baylor administrators later changed course and offered more of this theological justification.[7] When R1 status was eventually achieved, President Livingstone declared, "As a Christian university, there are not a lot of those among the R1 universities that are not only doing the highest level of research in the country but also maintaining the integrity of their Christian missions and thinking about how our faith community, our faith perspective informs the research we're doing and informs how we solve problems. . . . It's just really important to us on so many levels."[8]

A major difference between how Christ-assumed versus Christ-animating administrators approach goals is the scope by which they measure success. Christ-assumed administrators assume the spiritual health of those within the institution. Christ-animating administrators understand that the spiritual health of students, staff, and faculty is of primary importance, as we discuss in the following sections.

Students

First, how do you or how does your institution evaluate the success of your students? We find many Christian administrators employ the same metrics as secular institutions: retention rates, sense of belonging, and five-year graduation rates. Yet instead of focusing solely or primarily on student retention because it is an important *U.S. News & World Report* metric, Christian administrators should take a holistic approach to student flourishing. Do your measures of student success move beyond institutional self-interest to encompass the spiritual and moral health of students? We have ways to measure their well-being in these areas.[9]

Staff

Second, in a recent national study of student affairs staff, when we asked the question "How would you say your institution supports the Christian formation of employees in general?" one-third of our interviewees gave answers such as the following:

- "Hmm. Pass. [pause] It's not built into the culture where I'm at. It could be, it's just they have not done it."

- "Honestly, I don't know. I don't know that I've really seen [my institution] doing anything specifically for the spiritual development of their employees. I can't think of [pause], honestly, nothing comes to mind."
- "Not as much as I would expect from an institution so closely tied with the church."
- "So, besides our HR interview when we first came in, where they asked your statement of faith, I have never been asked about my church commitment or my involvement or any of that."[10]

In other words, student life administrators on these campuses either did not have a goal to help their staff grow as Christians in their jobs (or life in general) or simply were not accountable for doing so. Furthermore, staff did not experience accountability regarding the Christian mission. Student life experts in administration need to form a senior team to provide expert feedback to staff regarding whether they are fulfilling the Christian mission (an essential element for accountability).

Faculty

Third, annual and tenure reviews of faculty may not have anything related to the Christian mission; or, if they do, assessment is largely reliant upon student evaluations of the integration of faith and learning in their teaching. In other words, we have nonexperts, who often view faith and learning as praying or giving a devotion before class, evaluating professors. Christian universities that hope to better operationalize their Christian missions could instead form a team of mentors and evaluators with expertise in classroom faith integration and pedagogy if they want to keep faculty accountable in this area. Moreover, these experts must take steps to learn how to incentivize such improvements.

Furthermore, administrators often have very clear metrics for meeting goals outlined in the strategic plan. They display these metrics—related to buildings, student enrollment, and general teaching and research priorities—at yearly faculty meetings. There is little confusion about these institutional priorities and how we might individually and collectively go about pursuing them. Yet institutions often do not have comparable goals and metrics related to the distinctive Christian mission. Thus, although the strategic plan of a Christian institution may have general goals that could be used to chart growth toward strengthening its Christian mission (e.g., "Our institution will continue to offer mission-centric faculty formation programs that shape how faculty envision their teaching, mentoring, and research"), one rarely, if ever, sees specific, measurable goals related to this general goal or other specific Christian goals. Christ-animating administration involves taking pleasure in the flourishing of students, staff, and faculty as well as reaching particular institutional goals. Christian administrators should celebrate the success of these groups more than their own success.

Incentive Structures for the Goals: Administrators, Faculty, and Staff

Unfortunately, we rarely hear about ways board members and/or senior administrators at all levels of the institution (e.g., VPs, deans, and chairs), faculty, and staff are incentivized or rewarded to meet specific goals related to the Christian mission. Indeed, we have come to think that the lack of incentives in general, and especially among mid-level administrators such as deans and chairs, is one of the greatest hindrances to fulfilling the Christian missions of Christian colleges and universities. If Christian institutions seek to embody their Christian missions, we believe they will need experts and leaders who can give higher education professionals advice and hold them accountable in this area.

We do not mean to imply that administrators avoid accountability to the Christian mission on purpose. After all, they, like most people, want to be successful in their jobs—which in this case involves administering a university. So why do boards, presidents, and upper-level administrators fail to build accountability structures for the administrators, faculty, and staff under their supervision for one of the most important ends of their work? We have come across five basic reasons.

First, much of the problem involves the fact that most Christian universities simply borrow the accountability structure of secular universities. Some institutions maintain no explicitly Christian evaluative measures (the Christ-assumed approach), and others simply add a single Christian question to an annual review or faculty evaluation (the Christ-added approach). Such approaches avoid the difficult task of rethinking their whole accountability and incentive structure. Yet there is a big difference between merely encouraging good teaching, research, and service and encouraging professors to engage in the "creation and redemption of learners and learning."[11] Most administrators know how to do the former but not the latter. Thus, most Christian institutions simply copy whatever the rest of the American universities are doing regarding annual reviews, Title IX, diversity, accreditation, and so on. At best, they might add a goal related to a Christian mission that lacks incentives.

The copying of goals leads to the second major problem. Often, administrators use secular means to achieve their ends. Sadly, academic administrators are often not very academic about the means they use to achieve their ends. To increase their competence, administrators need to do the hard work of researching to find the best means for accomplishing their ends, in full consideration of the Christian mission of their institution, instead of merely copying other institutions.

Third, administrators allow the minimizing of human depravity to dominate their attention. They tend to focus on preventing bad things from happening (e.g., getting sued for a Title IX problem; receiving unwanted national media attention) versus encouraging good things (e.g., sex education classes that set forth a robust, positive Christian vision of and discussion about sexuality). Regarding the latter, a colleague of ours recently interviewed eighty-five Christian Title IX coordinators and found none of these institutions offered such a class on their campuses.[12] On these campuses, the structures for adjudicating sin were present, but the creative administrative structures for positive Christian education were lacking.[13]

Fourth, administrators fail to show humility by searching for advice from people who are competent regarding how to implement the Christian mission in specific ways. For example, during this research, we evaluated the presidential leadership teams of all the Protestant universities in the United States and almost always found individuals with expertise in finance, human resources, athletics, student affairs, and diversity. Yet as previous chapters demonstrated, only 17 percent of institutions had a vice president for mission or chaplains on that leadership team (for Catholic institutions, it was close to 50 percent). Most institutional leadership teams include no one with any formal theological education—no experts in this area. This observation raises questions about both the expertise and the ordering of loves at these Protestant institutions, many of which claim to be quite serious about the Christian mission. Once again, they are more apt to copy the latest trends regarding leadership teams (the latest is adding VPs of diversity, equity, and inclusion) than establishing a source of expertise for accountability to the Christian mission.

Finally, administrators fail to set up incentive structures that reward student, staff, and faculty development regarding the Christian mission. A love for Christ-animating learning is not easily compelled. Thus, the best approach is to provide incentives and rewards. Unfortunately, administrators are not known for their generous incentives generally, let alone for pursuits that further the Christian mission. As the satirical Associate Deans site recently tweeted, "It is that time of year when the college wants to thank all our faculty and staff for their hard work this year. Not with money, support, or resources. Not even with a catered luncheon. But with words in an email to the college listserv! Thanks for all you do!"[14] Thank-you notes are nice, but free lunches, free books, cash, and course releases prove to be more effective when demonstrating priorities. These incentives can be small, but they demonstrate that the institution notices and cares about student, staff, and faculty development for the Christian mission.

Likewise, it is important to demonstrate through financial incentives that the Christian mission is important to the institution. It is hardly surprising that institutions without financial or other incentives for Christ-animating scholarship, teaching, service, and student life programming struggle to find evidence of a Christian mission enacted on their campuses. What if institutions considered the Christian mission as a key facet of their faculty development efforts? In addition to the various grants, funding, and teaching and scholarship awards devoted to faculty development—as it is traditionally understood—a school could reward faculty who enact the Christian mission in particular ways. Faculty and staff could receive rewards for publishing Christ-animating scholarship or publishing in journals that feature such scholarship. New awards could be established to highlight the best Christ-animating teaching, and new incentives could encourage full-time faculty to attend workshops that teach them how to enhance Christ-animating teaching. Unfortunately, it is too often assumed that faculty do not need incentives to pursue specific means of strengthening or demonstrating the Christian mission of the institution. This assumption is particularly true for post-tenured faculty, toward whom few incentives are directed to encourage or engage them in mentoring younger faculty related to the Christian mission.[15]

Likewise, a lack of meaningful mentoring has been frequently cited in literature exploring the particularly high attrition of new student affairs professionals.[16] The absence of meaningful mentorship among staff likely evidences a comparable lack of institutional incentives for more experienced staff members to take on the time-consuming task of mentoring young professionals. Moreover, institutions often fail to allocate sufficient or, in some cases, any funding for staff and student professionals to develop their intellectual and practical competencies in other ways (conferences, scholarships, etc.). Of course, then, the inability of an institution to socialize staff members in how they might bring a Christian identity to bear on their professional practice via mentorship cannot be remedied independently, even by particularly growth-minded staff members. Moreover, even in institutions that offer incentives for the professional development of staff, administrators must ask, Do the incentives offered contribute to or potentially compete with distinctively Christian practice? For instance, do we discourage young staff members from attending a seemingly "less scholarly" conference centered on Christian thought and practice in favor of a more intellectually rigorous national conference aligned with institutional prestige rankings? Surely there are benefits to both conferences, but the point here is that our incentives speak volumes about our goals.

Accountability Mechanisms

We contest that if you are not trying to measure your progress toward a goal, you probably do not care much about it. At present, there are a host of social science measures advanced enough to afford administrators and faculty the ability to dismiss the excuse we most commonly hear: "Well, we really cannot measure the spiritual aspects of what we do." Yes, you actually can. Higher education scholars frequently do assess things far more subjective or ambiguous than "spirituality" or "character." Both quantitative and qualitative methods have been developed to allow us to do just that in a myriad of valid and reliable ways. For instance, a vast array of interview and focus-group approaches have long since afforded qualitative researchers insights into such variables. More recently, the development of psychometric scales in quantitative research allows scholar-practitioners to numerically present findings in ways sometimes more conducive to benchmarking and concise reporting. Therefore, the excuse that one cannot measure the spiritual aspects of what one does is little more than an attempt to protect one's own time. Thus, "Why should we measure such things?" is a far better question than "Can we measure such things?"

Christian administration assessment should be characterized by both measuring and reporting—in open meetings—not just on the well-being of the institution but on the health of faculty, staff, and students in as holistic a manner as possible. Special attention should be given to their spiritual well-being. In other words, Christian administrators should widen the metrics they use, making sure they measure those that serve not just the interests of the institution but also the interests of groups served by and within the institution.

Such reporting would require administrators to face some hard realities within a context of accountability. For instance, reporting that your institution received one of the lowest scores within higher education in a ranking of "best Christian workplaces" would require subsequent reporting on what you're doing to address that matter. Your metrics are how your institution is held accountable to its mission and espoused values.

So if you want to know whether an institution is serious about its Christian mission, ask this simple question: What are the leaders doing to increase the competence of the board and upper administrators regarding the Christian mission so they can exercise the virtue of accountability?

CONCLUSION

At the heart of this final chapter is our conviction that the truest loves of an institution can be ascertained by looking at its goals, its rationale for meeting those goals, the policies and incentive systems created to reach those goals, and its accountability structures for reporting results. Consequently, to understand the diversity of Christian universities, we provided an analysis of them that relied upon specific empirical measures (the OCIG). Our findings reveal not only that there are a diversity of denominational and nondenominational Christian institutions in America but that those institutions operationalize their Christian identity in a myriad of ways. We believe our findings can equip readers with more informed decision-making and stewardship of resources—personally or institutionally—as they move forward in their role, whether that be as a parent, staff member, faculty member, administrator, or board member. Our hope for you, our reader, is that this guide helps you understand the vast and often confusing landscape of Christian higher education.

Acknowledgments

This volume would not have been possible without significant support from others involved in this massive undertaking. This work was also supported by the following graduate students: Hina Abel, Rylie Ackley, Scott Alexander, Dana Christenson, Meghan Fletcher, Pacey Ham, Kara Hanson, Katie Klingstedt, Micah Mitchell, Rachel Olson, and Andrea Pouso Morales. Thanks for all of your help with this project.

Perry—I dedicate this book to my boys, Bennett and Cody, who attended or are attending Christian higher education. I'm so proud of you and the men you have become.

Ted—I dedicate this book to Steve Ivester, David Setran, and Dan Haase. They are winsome, godly mentors and friends who embody the very best of what Christian higher education has to offer. Thanks to each of you for the time and encouragement you have poured into me, but also for the intentionality and faithfulness with which you approach Christ-animated learning.

Jess—I dedicate this book to my parents. Thank you for faithfully encouraging me as I considered a Christian university initially as a high school student and again when I decided to go to graduate school. I think it is fair to say the world of Christian higher education caught us by surprise (in the best way). What was once a foreign landscape to us both has since become my vocational home!

List of Christian Colleges by OCIG Total

The following lists provide the scores of various groups of institutions by combining our scores into four general categories: 1. Rhetoric, 2. Membership, 3. Curricular, and 4. Co-Curricular. The categories include the following scores:

Rhetoric
- Protestant denominational or Catholic order identity, as well as Christian identity, affirmed in mission statement (2)
- Mission statement says they are "affiliated" with a certain denomination but does not provide any additional signifying Christian language or identity as Christian (1)
- Home page rhetoric of the web site exhibits Christian language (1)
- The "About Us" page contains explicitly Christian or explicitly denominational identification (1)

Membership
- Christian identity requirements for students (1)
- Christian identity or belief requirements for faculty (1 for all or 0.5 if part)
- Christian identity or belief requirements for staff (1)
- Christian identity or membership requirements for the president (1)
- Christian/church/denominational/order requirements for being on the governance board (1 for all or 0.5 if part)
- Vice-President for Mission or Chaplain included on Executive Leadership Team (1)

Curricular
- Specific Christian academic department (1)
- Number of required Christian classes (1-10)
- Explicitly Christian Centers or Institutes (1)

Co-Curricular
- Required chapel/mass (2) or Voluntary university chapel/mass privileged (1).
- Only Christian student groups exist on campus (1).
- Christian covenant (2), Christian reasoning (2), or Christianity mentioned (1) in the student conduct code.

In addition, in some tables the institutions are labeled according to the groups we used to divide our chapters. The following acronyms are used for the various groups.

C	Catholic
CCCU	Council For Christian Colleges and Universities
CC&IA	both CCCU and IACE
HBCU	Historically Black Colleges and Universities
IACE	International Association for Christian Education
LCP	Low Church Protestant
MLP	Mainline Protestant
EO	Eastern Orthodox

Finally, if you wish to see the more detailed scoring, you can visit: https://guide.perryglanzer.com/schools/

Top Scoring Schools by Classification

These lists provide the top 20% of institutions (or close to that percentage) by Christian tradition classification.

Top Scoring Catholic Institutions

NAME	RHETORIC	MEMBERSHIP	CURRICULAR	CO-CURRIC	TOTAL
John Paul the Great Catholic Univ.	4	4	11	4	23
Christendom College	4	2.5	10	4	20.5
Wyoming Catholic College	3	4.5	8	5	20.5
Magdalen College	3	3.5	8	5	19.5
Thomas Aquinas College	3	4	9	3	19
Thomas More College of Liberal Arts	4	3.5	8	3	18.5
Benedictine College	4	3.5	5	4	16.5
Ave Maria University	4	4	5	3	16
Franciscan University	4	3	5	4	16
Thomas More University	4	3.5	4	4	15.5
University of Notre Dame	4	3.5	5	3	15.5
Carroll College	4	3	6	2	15
Villanova University	4	3	5	3	15
Creighton University	4	3	4	3	14
Emmanuel College (MA)	3	3	5	3	14
Providence College	4	3	4	3	14
Saint John's University (NY)	4	3	5	2	14
Saint Leo University	4	3	4	3	14
Saint Mary's University (MN)	3	3	6	2	14
Santa Clara University	3	3	5	3	14
Saint Leo University	4	3	4	3	14
The Catholic University of America	3	3	4	4	14

Top Scoring CCCU/IACE Institutions

NAME	RHETORIC	MEMBERSHIP	CURRICULAR	CO-CURRIC	TOTAL
Biola University	4	5	12	5	26
Cairn University	4	5	11	5	25
Clarks Summit University	4	5	11	5	25
Life Pacific University	4	5	11	5	25
Montana Christian College	4	5	11	5	25
Ozark Christian College	4	5	11	5	25
Crown College	4	6	9	5	24
MidAtlantic Christian University	4	5	9	5	23
Southeastern University	4	6	8	5	23
Arizona Christian University	4	5	8	5	22
Kuyper College	4	5	8	5	22
North Central University	4	6	7	5	22
Taylor University	4	6	7	5	22
University of Northwestern-St. Paul	4	5	8	5	22
Welch College	4	4	11	3	22
Wheaton College (IL)	4	5	8	5	22
Alliance University	4	6	6	5	21
Cedarville University	4	6	6	5	21
Columbia International University	4	5	7	5	21
Covenant College	4	6	6	5	21
Criswell College	4	5	7	5	21
Grace Christian University	4	5	7	5	21
Johnson University (FL)	4	6	6	5	21
Multnomah University	4	5	7	5	21
Providence Christian College	4	5	7	5	21
William Jessup University	4	4	8	5	21
Azusa Pacific University	4	4	7	5	20
Faulkner University	4	4	7	5	20

NAME	RHETORIC	MEMBERSHIP	CURRICULAR	CO-CURRIC	TOTAL
Grace College (IN)	4	6	5	5	20
Montreat College	4	4	7	5	20
Toccoa Falls College	4	5	6	5	20
University of Valley Forge	4	5	6	5	20
Vanguard University	3	5	7	5	20
Whitworth University	4	5	7	4	20

Top Scoring HBCU Institutions

NAME	RHETORIC	MEMBERSHIP	CURRICULAR	CO-CURRIC	TOTAL
Simmons College of KY	4	5	10	3	22
Oakwood University	4	4	6	4	18
American Baptist College	4	3.5	4	3	14.5
Xavier University of Louisiana	3	1.5	4	3	11.5
Stillman College	1	0	5	5	11
Arkansas Baptist College	4	0.5	1	5	10.5
Edward Waters University	4	1	0	4	9
Voorhees College	4	0	1	4	9

Top Scoring Low-Church Protestant Institutions

NAME	RHETORIC	MEMBERSHIP	CURRICULAR	CO-CURRIC	TOTAL
Dallas Christian College	4	5	11	5	25
Great Lakes Christian College	4	5	11	5	25
Oak Hills Christian College	4	5	11	5	25
Spurgeon College	4	5	11	5	25
World Mission University	4	5	11	5	25
Arlington Baptist University	4	4	11	5	24
Boyce College	4	5	10	5	24

NAME	RHETORIC	MEMBERSHIP	CURRICULAR	CO-CURRIC	TOTAL
Calvary University	4	6	8	5	23
The Master's University	4	6	8	5	23
Ecclesia College	3	5	9	5	22
Bob Jones University	4	6	6	5	21
Baptist University of the Americas	4	5	6	5	20
Liberty University	4	5	7	4	20
Pillar College	4	4	8	4	20
Randall University	4	5	6	5	20
Trinity Baptist College	4	6	5	5	20

Top Scoring Mainline Protestant Institutions

NAME	RHETORIC	MEMBERSHIP	CURRICULAR	CO-CURRIC	TOTAL
Oklahoma Wesleyan University	4	4	5	5	18
Barclay College	4	2	3	5	14
University of Sioux Falls	3	4	3	4	14
Concordia University (St. Paul, MN)	4	3	4	2	13
Concordia University (TX)	4	4	1	4	13
Waynesburg University	4	4	2	2	12
Hope College	4	2.5	2	3	11.5
Huntingdon College	1	4	3	3	11
University of Dubuque	3	2	2	4	11
Bethel University (TN)	3	.5	1	4	8.5
Luther College	4	2.5	1	1	8.5
Valparaiso University	1	1.5	3	3	8.5
Bethany College (WV)	4	0	0	4	8
McMurry University	3	1	1	3	8
University of Jamestown	4	0	0	4	8
Ashland University	3	1.5	1	2	7.5

NAME	RHETORIC	MEMBERSHIP	CURRICULAR	CO-CURRIC	TOTAL
Gustavus Adolphus College	3	2.5	1	1	7.5
Wilmington College	2	1.5	1	3	7.5
Alderson-Broaddus University	2	0	1	4	7
Amridge University	3	0	2	2	7
Augsburg University	1	2	2	2	7
California Lutheran University	1	3	0	3	7
Newberry College	1	2	0	4	7
Concordia College (Moorehead, MN)	2	1.5	1	2	6.5
Texas Lutheran College	2	1.5	1	2	6.5
Tusculum University	2	1.5	1	2	6.5
William Penn University	1	0.5	2	3	6.5

Top Scoring Schools in Specific Categories

The following two charts list the top-scoring institutions in the two categories of membership and curriculum.

Top Scoring Institutions in Membership

Name	Group	Membership Score
Alliance University	CCCU	6
Bob Jones University	LCP	6
Calvary University	LCP	6
Cedarville University	IACE	6
Cornerstone University	CCCU	6
Covenant College	CCCU	6
Crown College	CCCU	6
Grace College (IN)	CC&IA	6
Johnson University (FL)	CCCU	6
North Central University	CCCU	6

Name	Group	Membership Score
Southeastern University	CCCU	6
Taylor University	CCCU	6
The Master's University	LCP	6
Trinity Baptist College	LCP	6

Top Scoring Institutions in Curriculum

Name	Group	Curriculum Score
Biola University	CC&IA	12
Briercrest College	CCCU	12
Arlington Baptist University	LCP	11
Cairn University	CC&IA	11
Clarks Summit University	CCCU	11
Dallas Christian College	LCP	11
Great Lakes Christian College	LCP	11
John Paul the Great Catholic University	C	11
Life Pacific University	CCCU	11
Montana Christian College	IACE	11
Oak Hills Christian College	LCP	11
Ozark Christian College	CCCU	11
Spurgeon College	LCP	11
Welch College	IACE	11
World Mission University	LCP	11
Boyce College	LCP	10
Christendom College	C	10
Simmons College of Kentucky	HBCU	10

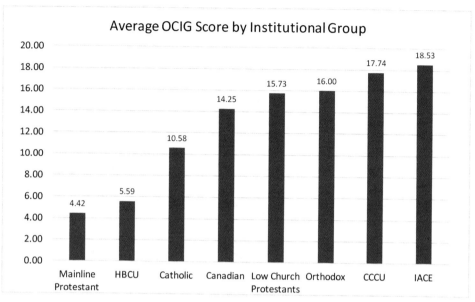

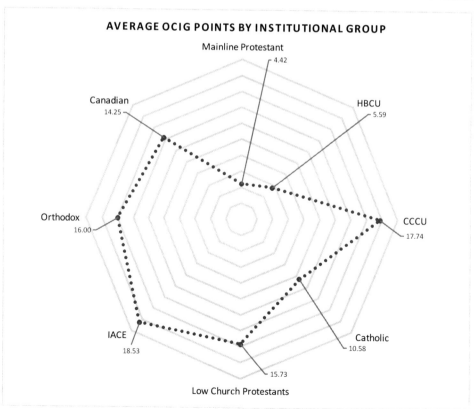

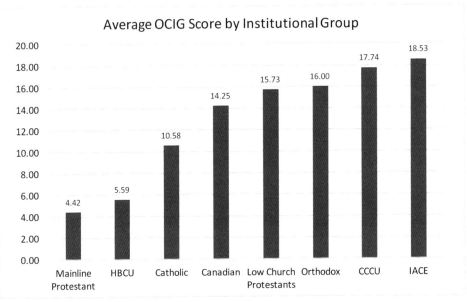

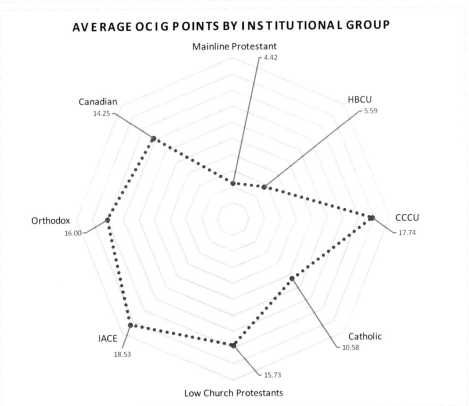

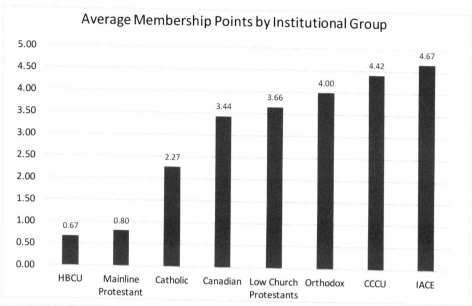

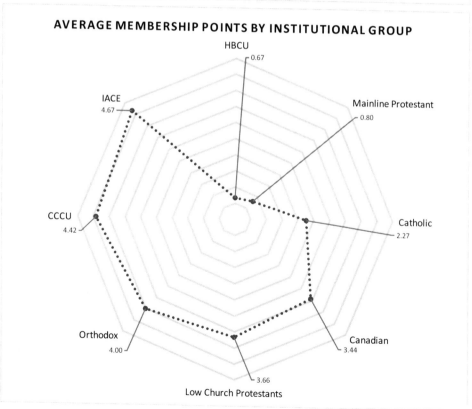

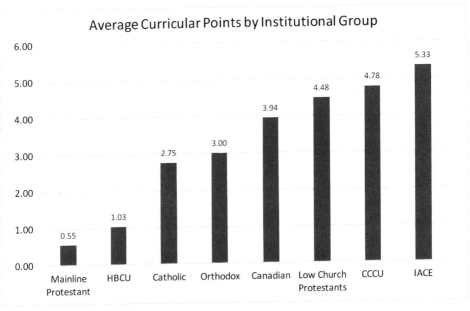

Average Curricular Points by Institutional Group

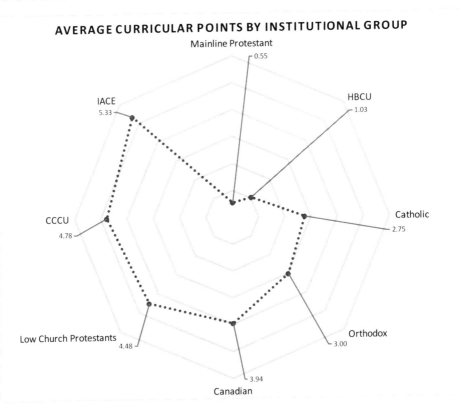

AVERAGE CURRICULAR POINTS BY INSTITUTIONAL GROUP

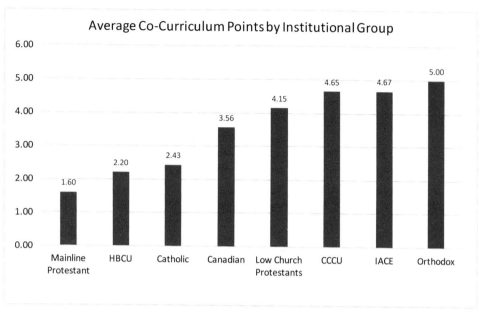

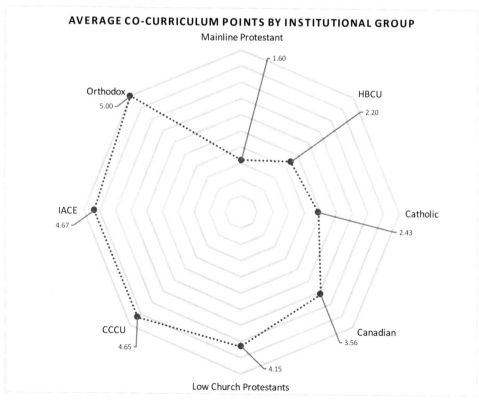

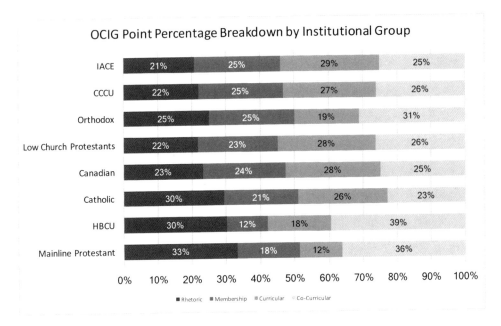

Listing of All American and Canadian Institutions by Total Score

NAME	TOTAL	NAME	TOTAL
Biola University	26	Wheaton College (IL)	22
Briercrest College	25	Alliance University	21
Cairn University	25	Bob Jones University	21
Clarks Summit University	25	Cedarville University	21
Dallas Christian College	25	Columbia International University	21
Great Lakes Christian College	25	Covenant College	21
Life Pacific University	25	Criswell College	21
Montana Christian College	25	Grace Christian University	21
Oak Hills Christian College	25	Johnson University	21
Ozark Christian College	25	Multnomah University	21
Spurgeon College	25	Providence Christian College	21
World Mission University	25	William Jessup University	21
Arlington Baptist University	24	Christendom College	20.5
Boyce College	24	Wyoming Catholic College	20.5
Crown College	24	Azusa Pacific University	20
Calvary University	23	Baptist University of the Americas	20
John Paul the Great Catholic University	23	Canadian Mennonite University	20
MidAtlantic Christian University	23	Faulkner University	20
Southeastern University	23	Grace College (IN)	20
The Master's University	23	Liberty University	20
Arizona Christian University	22	Montreat College	20
Ecclesia College	22	Pillar College	20
Kuyper College	22	Randall University	20
North Central University	22	Toccoa Falls College	20
Simmons College of Kentucky	22	Trinity Baptist College	20
Taylor University	22	University of Valley Forge	20
University of Northwestern-St. Paul	22	Vanguard University	20
Welch College	22	Whitworth University	20

NAME	TOTAL
Magdalen College	19.5
Abilene Christian University	19
Baptist College of Florida	19
Bryan College	19
Colorado Christian University	19
Corban University	19
Cornerstone University	19
George Fox University	19
Indiana Wesleyan University	19
Kentucky Christian University	19
LeTourneau University	19
Northwest Nazarene University	19
Northwest University	19
San Diego Christian College	19
Southwestern Christian University	19
Thomas Aquinas College	19
Trevecca Nazarene University	19
Trinity Western University	19
Truett McConnell University	19
Thomas More College of Liberal Arts	18.5
Ambrose University	18
Asbury University	18
Belhaven University	18
Bethesda University	18
Bushnell University	18
Dordt University	18
Emmanuel College (GA)	18
Gordon College	18
Grove City College	18

NAME	TOTAL
Houghton University	18
Huntington University	18
John Brown University	18
La Sierra University	18
Lee University	18
Lubbock Christian University	18
Malone University	18
Messiah University	18
Northwestern College (IA)	18
Oakwood University	18
Oklahoma Wesleyan University	18
Patrick Henry College	18
Point Loma Nazarene University	18
Point University	18
Seattle Pacific University	18
Simpson University (CA)	18
Southern Adventist University	18
Southwestern Assemblies of God University	18
Spring Arbor University	18
Tabor College	18
Trinity International University	18
Tyndale University	18
Walla Walla University	18
Westmont College	18
York University	18
Anderson University (SC)	17
Belmont University	17
Calvin University	17
Carson-Newman University	17

NAME	TOTAL
Central Baptist College	17
Concordia University (WI)	17
Crowley's Ridge College	17
Eastern University	17
Evangel University	17
Friends University	17
Hope International University	17
Houston Christian University	17
Lipscomb University	17
Loma Linda University	17
Mid-America Christian University	17
MidAmerica Nazarene University	17
Ohio Christian University	17
Providence	17
Regent University	17
Southwest Baptist University	17
Sterling College	17
Summit Christian College	17
Trinity Christian College	17
Union University	17
Warner Pacific University	17
Benedictine College	16.5
Andrews University	16
Ave Maria University	16
Bethel University (MN)	16
Bluffton University	16
California Baptist University	16
Charleston Southern University	16
College of the Ozarks	16

NAME	TOTAL
Concordia University (CA)	16
Concordia University (MI)	16
Dallas Baptist University	16
Eastern Mennonite University	16
Eastern Nazarene College	16
Florida College	16
Franciscan University	16
Fresno Pacific University	16
Geneva College	16
Greenville University	16
Hannibal-Lagrange College	16
Hardin Simmons University	16
Harding University	16
Hellenic College	16
Howard Payne University	16
Judson University	16
Kansas Christian College	16
Louisiana Christian University	16
Mississippi College	16
Missouri Baptist University	16
North Park University	16
Oklahoma Christian University	16
Redeemer University	16
Southern Nazarene University	16
Southern Wesleyan University	16
Southwestern Adventist University	16
The King's University	16
University of Mary Hardin-Baylor	16
University of Mobile	16

NAME	TOTAL
Warner University	16
Wayland Baptist University	16
Wisconsin Lutheran College	16
Thomas More University	15.5
University of Notre Dame	15.5
Anderson University (IN)	15
Bethel University (IN)	15
Blue Mountain College	15
Bluefield University	15
Booth University College	15
Carroll College	15
Concordia University (NE)	15
Crandall University	15
East Texas Baptist University	15
Erskine College	15
Freed-Hardeman University	15
King University	15
Milligan College	15
Mount Vernon Nazarene University	15
New Saint Andrews College	15
North Greenville University	15
Oklahoma Baptist University	15
Olivet Nazarene University	15
Oral Roberts University	15
Ouachita Baptist University	15
Pacific Union College	15
Palm Beach Atlantic University	15
Rochester College	15
Samford University	15

NAME	TOTAL
Villanova University	15
Williams Baptist University	15
American Baptist College	14.5
Grand Canyon University	14.5
Barclay College	14
Bethany Lutheran College	14
Brewton-Parker College	14
Campbell University	14
Concordia University (IL)	14
Creighton University	14
Emmanuel College (MA)	14
Hesston College	14
Providence College	14
Roberts Wesleyan College	14
Saint John's University	14
Saint Leo University	14
Saint Mary's University (MN)	14
Santa Clara University	14
Shorter University (GA)	14
The Catholic University of America	14
Union College	14
University of Sioux Falls	14
University of the Southwest	14
Aquinas College (TN)	13.5
Belmont Abbey College	13.5
Boston College	13.5
Caldwell University	13.5
DeSales University	13.5
Gardner-Webb University	13.5

NAME	TOTAL
King's College	13.5
Saint Thomas University (FL)	13.5
Saint Vincent College	13.5
Assumption University	13
Baylor University	13
Burman University	13
Carolina University	13
Central Christian College	13
Concordia University (St. Paul, MN)	13
Concordia University (TX)	13
Dominican University	13
Goshen University	13
Los Angeles Pacific University	13
Mount St. Mary's University (MD)	13
Pepperdine University	13
Saint Anselm College	13
Saint John's University	13
Saint Norbert College	13
University of Dayton	13
University of Fort Lauderdale	13
University of Portland	13
University of Providence	13
University of Scranton	13
Xavier University	13
Barry University	12.5
Briar Cliff University	12.5
Loyola University Maryland	12.5
Loyola Marymount University	12.5
Marymount University	12.5

NAME	TOTAL
Newman University	12.5
Oakland City University	12.5
University of Mary	12.5
Alvernia University	12
Campbellsville University	12
Gonzaga University	12
Lewis University	12
Lourdes University	12
Marian University (IN)	12
Mount Mary University	12
Ohio Dominican University	12
Saint Joseph's College of Maine	12
Saint Mary's University (TX)	12
Stonehill College	12
University of Dallas	12
University of Saint Thomas (TX)	12
Waynesburg University	12
Brescia University	11.5
Canisius College	11.5
College of Saint Benedict	11.5
Hope College	11.5
Mount Marty College	11.5
Regis University	11.5
Saint Joseph's University	11.5
Saint Mary's College	11.5
Saint Peter's University	11.5
William Carey University	11.5
Xavier University of Louisiana	11.5
Benedictine University	11

NAME	TOTAL
Chaminade University of Honolulu	11
College of Saint Scholastica	11
Gannon University	11
Holy Family University	11
Huntingdon College	11
Marquette University	11
Mercyhurst University	11
Saint Bonaventure University	11
Seton Hall University	11
Stillman College	11
University of Dubuque	11
University of Saint Francis (IL)	11
University of Saint Thomas (MN)	11
University of the Cumberlands	11
Anna Maria College	10.5
Arkansas Baptist College	10.5
Franciscan Missionaries of Our Lady Univ.	10.5
Georgetown College	10.5
Immaculata University	10.5
King's University College	10.5
Marian University (WI)	10.5
Our Lady of the Lake University	10.5
Saint Catherine University	10.5
Salve Regina University	10.5
Seton Hill University	10.5
Spring Hill College	10.5
Viterbo University	10.5
Aquinas College (MI)	10
Calumet College of St. Joseph	10

NAME	TOTAL
Chowan University	10
College of Saint Mary	10
Fairfield University	10
Hilbert College	10
La Roche University	10
Loras College	10
Loyola University Chicago	10
Niagara University	10
Rivier University	10
Saint Mary's College of California	10
Siena College	10
University of Detroit Mercy	10
Walsh University	10
Washington Adventist University	10
Wheeling University	10
College of the Holy Cross	9.5
Iona College	9.5
Le Moyne College	9.5
Marywood University	9.5
Neumann University	9.5
Notre Dame College	9.5
Rockhurst University	9.5
Saint Michael's College	9.5
University of Saint Francis (IN)	9.5
University of the Incarnate Word	9.5
Villa Maria College of Buffalo	9.5
Carlow University	9
Donnelly College	9
Duquesne University	9

NAME	TOTAL
Edward Waters College	9
Fordham University	9
Madonna University	9
Manhattan College	9
Molloy University	9
Mount Aloysius College	9
Saint Ambrose University	9
Saint Francis University	9
University of Holy Cross	9
University of San Diego	9
University of San Francisco	9
Voorhees College	9
Avila University	8.5
Bellarmine University	8.5
Bethel University (TN)	8.5
Bethune-Cookman University	8.5
Elms College	8.5
Georgetown University	8.5
John Carroll University	8.5
Luther College	8.5
Sacred Heart University	8.5
Saint Elizabeth University	8.5
Seattle University	8.5
Trinity University	8.5
University of Saint Joseph	8.5
Valparaiso University	8.5
Amberton University	8
Bethany College (WV)	8
Dominican College of Blauvelt	8

NAME	TOTAL
Georgian Court University	8
Gwynedd-Mercy University	8
Jarvis Christian College	8
La Salle University	8
Loyola University New Orleans	8
Manor College	8
McMurry University	8
Merrimack College	8
Mount Saint Mary College	8
Regis College	8
Saint Edward's University	8
Saint Louis University	8
University of Jamestown	8
University of Mount Olive	8
University of Saint Mary	8
Albertus Magnus College	7.5
Alverno College	7.5
Ashland University	7.5
De Paul University	7.5
Gustavus Adolphus College	7.5
Maria College	7.5
Paine College	7.5
Saint Martin's University	7.5
Saint Xavier University	7.5
Wilmington College	7.5
Alderson-Broaddus University	7
Amridge University	7
Augsburg University	7
Berea College	7

NAME	TOTAL	NAME	TOTAL
Cabrini University	7	Paul Quinn College	6
California Lutheran University	7	Westminster College (PA)	6
Edgewood College	7	Bethel College (KS)	5.5
Fontbonne University	7	Christian Brothers University	5.5
Mars Hill University	7	Clarke University	5.5
Mount Mercy College	7	Mount Saint Mary's University (CA)	5.5
Newberry College	7	Notre Dame de Namur University	5.5
Quincy University	7	Philander Smith College	5.5
Rosemont College	7	Saint Augustine's College	5.5
Saint Mary-of-the-Woods College	7	Saint Mary's University (Canada)	5.5
Saint Paul University	7	Saint Olaf College	5.5
Saint Thomas Aquinas College	7	Saint Thomas University (Canada)	5.5
Siena Heights University	7	University of Indianapolis	5.5
Chestnut Hill College	6.5	Wartburg College	5.5
College of Mount Saint Vincent	6.5	Berry College	5
Concordia College (Moorehead, MN)	6.5	Catawba College	5
Felician University	6.5	Grand View University	5
Mercy College of Ohio	6.5	Greensboro College	5
Saint Jerome's University	6.5	Tennessee Wesleyan University	5
Texas Lutheran College	6.5	University of Pikeville	5
Tusculum University	6.5	University of the Ozarks	5
Ursuline College	6.5	Waldorf University	5
William Penn University	6.5	Carthage College	4.5
Augustana University (SD)	6	Kansas Wesleyan University	4.5
D'Youville College	6	LaGrange College	4.5
Emory and Henry College	6	Lane College	4.5
Hillsdale College	6	Lenoir-Rhyne University	4.5
Misericordia University	6	Lindsey Wilson College	4.5
Ottawa University	6	Lyon College	4.5

NAME	TOTAL
Morris Brown College	4.5
Mount Saint Joseph	4.5
Nebraska Wesleyan University	4.5
Oklahoma City University	4.5
Pfeiffer University	4.5
Presbyterian College	4.5
Virginia Union University	4.5
West Virginia Wesleyan College	4.5
Allen University	4
Austin College	4
Eureka College	4
Hastings College	4
Limestone University	4
Saint Andrews University	4
Texas College	4
Wingate University	4
Adrian College	3.5
Augustana College (IL)	3.5
Capital University	3.5
Centenary College of Louisiana	3.5
Central Methodist University	3.5
Clinton College	3.5
College of Saint Rose	3.5
Davidson College	3.5
Earlham College	3.5
North Carolina Wesleyan College	3.5
Rust College	3.5
Sewanee: University of the South	3.5
Spalding University	3.5

NAME	TOTAL
Thiel College	3.5
Wittenberg University	3.5
Carroll University	3
Claflin University	3
Defiance College	3
Dillard University	3
Kentucky Wesleyan College	3
Lakeland University	3
Maryville College	3
McPherson College	3
Midland University	3
Pacific Lutheran University	3
The University of Findlay	3
Virginia University of Lynchburg	3
Wiley College	3
William Woods University	3
Haverford College	2.5
Hendrix College	2.5
Huston-Tillotson University	2.5
Muhlenberg College	2.5
Ohio Northern University	2.5
Piedmont University	2.5
Roanoke College	2.5
Rocky Mountain College	2.5
Schreiner University	2.5
Shenandoah University	2.5
Virginia Wesleyan University	2.5
Baker University	2
Birmingham-Southern College	2

NAME	TOTAL
Dakota Wesleyan University	2
Fisk University	2
Hanover College	2
LeMoyne-Owen College	2
Livingstone College	2
McKendree University	2
Morris College	2
Muskingum University	2
Shaw University	2
Spelman College	2
University of Tulsa	2
Wesleyan College (GA)	2
Wilberforce University	2
Wilson College	2
Bennett College	1.5
College of Wooster	1.5
Ferrum College	1.5
Hamline University	1.5
High Point University	1.5
Manchester University	1.5
Methodist University	1.5

NAME	TOTAL
Moravian University	1.5
Ohio Wesleyan University	1.5
Simpson College (IA)	1.5
Alma College	1
Bacone College	1
Benedict College	1
Bethany College (KS)	1
Bloomfield College	1
Brevard College	1
Buena Vista University	1
Davis & Elkins College	1
Guilford College	1
Johnson C. Smith University	1
Lebanon Valley College	1
Lindenwood University	1
North Central College	1
Southwestern University	1
Texas Wesleyan University	1
Tougaloo College	1
University of Lynchburg	1

Alphabetical Listing of All American and Canadian Schools with Their Score Categories

NAME	RHETORIC	MEMBERSHIP	CURRICULAR	CO-CURRIC	TOTAL
Abilene Christian University	4	4	6	5	19
Adrian College	1	0.5	0	2	3.5
Albertus Magnus College	4	1.5	0	2	7.5
Alderson-Broaddus University	2	0	1	4	7
Allen University	0	0	1	3	4
Alliance University	4	6	6	5	21
Alma College	0	0	0	1	1
Alvernia University	3	3	2	4	12
Alverno College	3	1.5	0	3	7.5
Amberton University	2	4	0	2	8
Ambrose University	4	4	5	5	18
American Baptist College	4	3.5	4	3	14.5
Amridge University	3	0	2	2	7
Anderson University (IN)	4	4	3	4	15
Anderson University (SC)	4	5	3	5	17
Andrews University	2	4	5	5	16
Anna Maria College	3	1.5	3	3	10.5
Aquinas College (MI)	4	1	2	3	10
Aquinas College (TN)	3	3.5	5	2	13.5
Arizona Christian University	4	5	8	5	22
Arkansas Baptist College	4	0.5	1	5	10.5
Arlington Baptist University	4	4	11	5	24
Asbury University	4	4	5	5	18
Ashland University	3	1.5	1	2	7.5
Assumption University	3	2	4	4	13
Augsburg University	1	2	2	2	7
Augustana College (IL)	1	1.5	0	1	3.5

NAME	RHETORIC	MEMBERSHIP	CURRICULAR	CO-CURRIC	TOTAL
Augustana University (SD)	2	1	2	1	6
Austin College	2	0	0	2	4
Ave Maria University	4	4	5	3	16
Avila University	3	1.5	1	3	8.5
Azusa Pacific University	4	4	7	5	20
Bacone College	0	0	1	0	1
Baker University	1	0	0	1	2
Baptist College of Florida	4	5	5	5	19
Baptist University of the Americas	4	5	6	5	20
Barclay College	4	2	3	5	14
Barry University	3	2.5	5	2	12.5
Baylor University	4	2	3	4	13
Belhaven University	4	4	6	4	18
Bellarmine University	3	1.5	3	1	8.5
Belmont Abbey College	3	2.5	4	4	13.5
Belmont University	4	5	4	4	17
Benedict College	0	0	0	1	1
Benedictine College	4	3.5	5	4	16.5
Benedictine University	4	2	4	1	11
Bennett College	1	0.5	0	0	1.5
Berea College	3	0	1	3	7
Berry College	3	0	0	2	5
Bethany College (KS)	0	0	0	1	1
Bethany College (WV)	4	0	0	4	8
Bethany Lutheran College	4	4	2	4	14
Bethel College (KS)	2	.5	1	2	5.5
Bethel University (IN)	4	4	3	4	15
Bethel University (MN)	3	4	4	5	16
Bethel University (TN)	3	.5	1	4	8.5
Bethesda University	3	4	6	5	18

NAME	RHETORIC	MEMBERSHIP	CURRICULAR	CO-CURRIC	TOTAL
Bethune-Cookman University	3	0.5	2	3	8.5
Biola University	4	5	12	5	26
Birmingham-Southern College	1	0	0	1	2
Bloomfield College	0	0	0	1	1
Blue Mountain College	3	4	3	5	15
Bluefield University	3	4	3	5	15
Bluffton University	4	4	4	4	16
Bob Jones University	4	6	6	5	21
Booth University College	4	4	3	4	15
Boston College	4	2.5	4	3	13.5
Boyce College	4	5	10	5	24
Brescia University	4	1.5	2	4	11.5
Brevard College	1	0	0	0	1
Brewton-Parker College	2	4	3	5	14
Briar Cliff University	3	2.5	4	3	12.5
Briarcrest College	4	4	12	5	25
Bryan College	4	4	6	5	19
Buena Vista University	0	0	0	1	1
Burman University	1	4	3	5	13
Bushnell University	4	4	6	4	18
Cabrini University	4	2	0	1	7
Cairn University	4	5	11	5	25
Caldwell University	4	1.5	6	2	13.5
California Baptist University	3	4	4	5	16
California Lutheran University	1	3	0	3	7
Calumet College of Saint Joseph	4	2	2	2	10
Calvary University	4	6	8	5	23
Calvin University	4	5	5	3	17
Campbell University	4	3	2	3	12
Campbellsville University	3	4	3	4	14

NAME	RHETORIC	MEMBERSHIP	CURRICULAR	CO-CURRIC	TOTAL
Canadian Mennonite University	3	4	8	5	20
Canisius College	4	1.5	3	3	11.5
Capital University	1	0.5	1	1	3.5
Carlow University	4	1	0	4	9
Carolina University	3	3	3	4	13
Carroll College	4	3	6	2	15
Carroll University	2	0	0	1	3
Carson-Newman University	4	5	3	5	17
Carthage College	2	1.5	0	1	4.5
Catawba College	2	0	1	2	5
Cedarville University	4	6	6	5	21
Centenary College of Louisiana	1	0.5	0	2	3.5
Central Baptist College	4	4	4	5	17
Central Christian College	3	4	2	4	13
Central Methodist University	1	0.5	0	2	3.5
Chaminade University of Honolulu	3	3	3	2	11
Charleston Southern University	4	4	3	5	16
Chestnut Hill College	3	1.5	0	2	6.5
Chowan University	4	2	1	3	10
Christendom College	4	2.5	10	4	20.5
Christian Brothers University	3	1.5	0	1	5.5
Claflin University	1	0	0	2	3
Clarke University	2	1.5	0	2	5.5
Clarks Summit University	4	5	11	5	25
Clinton College	1	0.5	0	2	3.5
College of Mount Saint Vincent	2	1.5	1	2	6.5
College of Saint Benedict	3	1.5	5	2	11.5
College of Saint Mary	3	2	3	2	10
College of Saint Rose	2	1.5	0	0	3.5
College of Saint Scholastica	4	3	3	1	11

NAME	RHETORIC	MEMBERSHIP	CURRICULAR	CO-CURRIC	TOTAL
College of the Holy Cross	3	1.5	3	2	9.5
Elms College	4	1.5	1	2	8.5
College of the Ozarks	4	4	3	5	16
College of Wooster	0	0.5	0	1	1.5
Colorado Christian University	4	5	5	5	19
Columbia International University	4	5	7	5	21
Concordia College (Moorehead, MN)	2	1.5	1	2	6.5
Concordia University (CA)	4	4	3	5	16
Concordia University (IL)	4	4	3	3	14
Concordia University (MI)	4	4	3	5	16
Concordia University (NE)	4	4	2	5	15
Concordia University (St. Paul, MN)	4	3	4	2	13
Concordia University (TX)	4	4	1	4	13
Concordia University (WI)	4	4	4	5	17
Corban University	4	5	5	5	19
Cornerstone University	4	6	4	5	19
Covenant College	4	6	6	5	21
Crandall University	4	4	4	3	15
Creighton University	4	3	4	3	14
Criswell College	4	5	7	5	21
Crowley's Ridge College	4	5	5	3	17
Crown College	4	6	9	5	24
Dakota Wesleyan University	1	0	0	1	2
Dallas Baptist University	4	4	3	5	16
Dallas Christian College	4	5	11	5	25
Davidson College	3	0.5	0	0	3.5
Davis & Elkins College	0	0	0	1	1
De Paul University	2	2.5	2	1	7.5
Defiance College	1	0	0	2	3
DeSales University	4	2.5	5	2	13.5

NAME	RHETORIC	MEMBERSHIP	CURRICULAR	CO-CURRIC	TOTAL
Dillard University	1	0	0	2	3
Dominican College of Blauvelt	3	2	0	3	8
Dominican University	3	3	6	1	13
Donnelly College	4	1	0	4	9
Dordt University	4	5	5	4	18
Duquesne University	3	2	3	1	9
D'Youville College	2	2	0	2	6
Earlham College	2	1.5	0	0	3.5
East Texas Baptist University	4	4	3	4	15
Eastern Mennonite University	4	2	5	5	16
Eastern Nazarene College	4	4	4	4	16
Eastern University	4	4	4	5	17
Ecclesia College	3	5	9	5	22
Edgewood College	3	2	0	2	7
Edward Waters College	4	1	0	4	9
Emmanuel College (GA)	4	4	5	5	18
Emmanuel College (MA)	3	3	5	3	14
Emory and Henry College	4	0	0	2	6
Erskine College	4	4	4	3	15
Eureka College	3	0	0	1	4
Evangel University	4	5	3	5	17
Fairfield University	4	2	1	3	10
Faulkner University	4	4	7	5	20
Felician University	1	2.5	1	2	6.5
Ferrum College	0	0.5	0	1	1.5
Fisk University	0	0	0	2	2
Florida College	4	4	3	5	16
Fontbonne University	3	2	0	2	7
Fordham University	3	3	2	1	9
Franciscan Missionaries of Our Lady U	4	2.5	2	2	10.5

NAME	RHETORIC	MEMBERSHIP	CURRICULAR	CO-CURRIC	TOTAL
Franciscan University	4	3	5	4	16
Freed-Hardeman University	4	4	4	3	15
Fresno Pacific University	4	5	3	4	16
Friends University	4	5	4	4	17
Gannon University	3	2	4	2	11
Gardner-Webb University	2	4.5	3	4	13.5
Geneva College	4	4	4	4	16
George Fox University	4	4	6	5	19
Georgetown College	4	1.5	1	4	10.5
Georgetown University	4	1.5	2	1	8.5
Georgian Court University	3	2	1	2	8
Gonzaga University	4	3	3	2	12
Gordon College	4	5	4	5	18
Goshen University	3	2	3	5	13
Grace Christian University	4	5	7	5	21
Grace College (IN)	4	6	5	5	20
Grand Canyon University	4	3.5	3	4	14.5
Grand View University	2	0	1	2	5
Great Lakes Christian College	4	5	11	5	25
Greensboro College	3	0	0	2	5
Greenville University	4	4	3	5	16
Grove City College	4	5	4	5	18
Guilford College	1	0	0	0	1
Gustavus Adolphus College	3	2.5	1	1	7.5
Gwynedd-Mercy University	3	3	0	2	8
Hamline University	1	0.5	0	0	1.5
Hannibal-Lagrange College	4	4	3	5	16
Hanover College	0	0	1	1	2
Hardin Simmons University	4	4	3	5	16
Harding University	4	4	5	5	18

NAME	RHETORIC	MEMBERSHIP	CURRICULAR	CO-CURRIC	TOTAL
Hastings College	2	0	0	2	4
Haverford College	1	0.5	0	1	2.5
Hellenic College	4	4	3	5	16
Hendrix College	1	0.5	0	1	2.5
Hesston College	4	3	2	5	14
High Point University	0	0.5	0	1	1.5
Hilbert College	3	3	2	2	10
Hillsdale College	3	0	1	2	6
Holy Family University	3	3	1	4	11
Hope College	4	2.5	2	3	11.5
Hope International University	4	4	4	5	17
Houghton University	4	5	4	5	18
Houston Christian University	4	4	4	5	17
Howard Payne University	4	4	3	5	16
Huntingdon College	1	4	3	3	11
Huntington University	4	5	4	5	18
Huston-Tillotson University	1	0.5	0	1	2.5
Immaculata University	3	2.5	3	2	10.5
Indiana Wesleyan University	4	5	5	5	19
Iona College	3	1.5	1	4	9.5
Jarvis Christian College	4	1	0	3	8
John Brown University	4	4	5	5	18
John Carroll University	3	2.5	2	1	8.5
John Paul the Great Catholic Univ.	4	4	11	4	23
Johnson C. Smith University	0	0	0	1	1
Johnson University	4	6	6	5	21
Judson University	4	4	3	5	16
Kansas Christian College	4	5	2	5	16
Kansas Wesleyan University	2	0.5	0	2	4.5
Kentucky Christian University	4	4	7	4	19

NAME	RHETORIC	MEMBERSHIP	CURRICULAR	CO-CURRIC	TOTAL
Kentucky Wesleyan College	1	0	0	2	3
King University	3	4	3	5	15
King's University College	4	2.5	1	3	10.5
King's College	4	1.5	6	2	13.5
Kuyper College	4	5	8	5	22
La Roche University	3	2	1	4	10
La Salle University	3	3	1	1	8
La Sierra University	4	4	5	5	18
LaGrange College	1	1.5	1	1	4.5
Lakeland University	1	0	0	2	3
Lane College	1	0.5	0	3	4.5
Le Moyne College	3	2.5	3	1	9.5
Lebanon Valley College	0	0	0	1	1
Lee University	4	4	5	5	18
LeMoyne-Owen College	0	0	0	2	2
Lenoir-Rhyne University	0	2.5	0	2	4.5
LeTourneau University	4	5	5	5	19
Lewis University	3	3	5	1	12
Liberty University	4	5	7	4	20
Life Pacific University	4	5	11	5	25
Limestone University	2	0	0	2	4
Lindenwood University	0	0	0	1	1
Lindsey Wilson College	2	0.5	0	2	4.5
Lipscomb University	4	4	4	5	17
Livingstone College	2	0	0	0	2
Loma Linda University	4	4	4	5	17
Loras College	3	2	4	1	10
Los Angeles Pacific University	4	4	3	2	13
Louisiana Christian University	4	4	3	5	16
Lourdes University	3	3	3	3	12

NAME	RHETORIC	MEMBERSHIP	CURRICULAR	CO-CURRIC	TOTAL
Loyola University Maryland	3	1.5	4	4	12.5
Loyola Marymount University	3	2.5	4	3	12.5
Loyola University Chicago	3	3	2	2	10
Loyola University New Orleans	3	2	2	1	8
Lubbock Christian University	4	4	5	5	18
Luther College	4	2.5	1	1	8.5
Lyon College	1	0.5	1	2	4.5
Madonna University	2	2	3	2	9
Magdalen College	3	3.5	8	5	19.5
Malone University	4	4	5	5	18
Manchester University	0	0.5	0	1	1.5
Manhattan College	3	3	1	2	9
Manor College	3	2	0	3	8
Maria College	3	2.5	0	2	7.5
Marian University (IN)	4	2	4	2	12
Marian University (WI)	4	1.5	2	3	10.5
Marquette University	4	3	3	1	11
Mars Hill University	3	1	1	2	7
Marymount University	3	1.5	5	3	12.5
Maryville College	0	0	0	3	3
Marywood University	3	2.5	2	2	9.5
McKendree University	1	0	0	1	2
McMurry University	3	1	1	3	8
McPherson College	1	0	0	2	3
Mercy College of Ohio	4	1.5	0	1	6.5
Mercyhurst University	2	2	3	4	11
Merrimack College	2	3	1	2	8
Messiah University	4	4	5	5	18
Methodist University	1	0.5	0	0	1.5
Mid-America Christian University	4	4	5	4	17

NAME	RHETORIC	MEMBERSHIP	CURRICULAR	CO-CURRIC	TOTAL
MidAmerica Nazarene University	4	4	4	5	17
MidAtlantic Christian University	4	5	9	5	23
Midland University	1	0	0	2	3
Milligan College	3	4	4	4	15
Misericordia University	2	2	0	2	6
Mississippi College	4	4	3	5	16
Missouri Baptist University	4	4	3	5	16
Molloy University	3	2	2	2	9
Montana Christian College	4	5	11	5	25
Montreat College	4	4	7	5	20
Moravian University	0	0.5	0	1	1.5
Morris Brown College	2	0.5	0	2	4.5
Morris College	0	1	0	1	2
Mount Aloysius College	3	2	1	3	9
Mount Marty College	4	2.5	3	2	11.5
Mount Mary University	2	3	5	2	12
Mount Mercy College	2	3	0	2	7
Mount Saint Joseph	2	1.5	0	1	4.5
Mount Saint Mary College	2	2	2	2	8
Mount Saint Mary's University (CA)	2	1.5	0	2	5.5
Mount Saint Mary's University (MD)	4	3	3	3	13
Mount Vernon Nazarene University	3	4	3	5	15
Muhlenberg College	1	0.5	0	1	2.5
Multnomah University	4	5	7	5	21
Muskingum University	0	0	0	2	2
Nebraska Wesleyan University	2	1.5	0	1	4.5
Neumann University	3	2.5	3	1	9.5
New Saint Andrews College	4	5	3	3	15
Newberry College	1	2	0	4	7
Newman University	4	1.5	3	4	12.5

NAME	RHETORIC	MEMBERSHIP	CURRICULAR	CO-CURRIC	TOTAL
Niagara University	3	3	3	1	10
North Carolina Wesleyan College	1	0.5	0	2	3.5
North Central College	0	0	0	1	1
North Central University	4	6	7	5	22
North Greenville University	3	4	3	5	15
North Park University	4	5	3	4	16
Northwest Nazarene University	4	5	5	5	19
Northwest University	4	5	5	5	19
Northwestern College (IA)	4	5	5	4	18
Notre Dame College	3	1.5	2	3	9.5
Notre Dame de Namur University	3	0.5	1	1	5.5
Oak Hills Christian College	4	5	11	5	25
Oakland City University	4	3.5	1	4	12.5
Oakwood University	4	4	6	4	18
Ohio Christian University	4	4	4	5	17
Ohio Dominican University	4	2	4	2	12
Ohio Northern University	1	0.5	0	1	2.5
Ohio Wesleyan University	1	0.5	0	0	1.5
Oklahoma Baptist University	3	4	3	5	15
Oklahoma Christian University	4	4	4	4	16
Oklahoma City University	2	0.5	1	1	4.5
Oklahoma Wesleyan University	4	4	5	5	18
Olivet Nazarene University	3	4	3	5	15
Oral Roberts University	4	4	3	4	15
Ottawa University	3	1	1	1	6
Ouachita Baptist University	4	4	3	4	15
Our Lady of the Lake University	4	2.5	2	2	10.5
Ozark Christian College	4	5	11	5	25
Pacific Lutheran University	1	0	1	1	3
Pacific Union College	4	2	7	2	15

NAME	RHETORIC	MEMBERSHIP	CURRICULAR	CO-CURRIC	TOTAL
Paine College	3	1.5	1	2	7.5
Palm Beach Atlantic University	3	5	3	4	15
Patrick Henry College	4	5	4	5	18
Paul Quinn College	3	0	1	2	6
Pepperdine University	4	2	4	3	13
Pfeiffer University	2	1.5	0	1	4.5
Philander Smith College	1	1.5	0	3	5.5
Piedmont University	0	1.5	0	1	2.5
Pillar College	4	4	8	4	20
Point Loma Nazarene University	4	5	4	5	18
Point University	4	4	6	4	18
Presbyterian College	2	0.5	2	0	4.5
Providence (Canada)	4	4	4	5	17
Providence Christian College	4	5	7	5	21
Providence College	4	3	4	3	14
Quincy University	2	2	1	2	7
Randall University	4	5	6	5	20
Redeemer University	4	4	4	4	16
Regent University	4	4	5	4	17
Regis College	2	2	0	4	8
Regis University	4	2.5	1	4	11.5
Rivier University	4	2	0	4	10
Roanoke College	1	0.5	0	1	2.5
Roberts Wesleyan College	4	4	2	4	14
Rochester College	4	4	4	3	15
Rockhurst University	2	2.5	2	3	9.5
Rocky Mountain College	1	0.5	0	1	2.5
Rosemont College	2	1	2	2	7
Rust College	1	0.5	0	2	3.5
Sacred Heart University	2	1.5	3	2	8.5

NAME	RHETORIC	MEMBERSHIP	CURRICULAR	CO-CURRIC	TOTAL
Saint Ambrose University	3	2	2	2	9
Saint Andrews University	0	3	0	1	4
Saint Anselm College	3	2	4	4	13
Saint Augustine's College	1	0.5	1	3	5.5
Saint Bonaventure University	2	2	4	3	11
Saint Catherine University	3	1.5	3	3	10.5
Saint Edward's University	3	2	2	1	8
Saint Elizabeth University	3	0.5	3	2	8.5
Saint Francis University	3	2	2	2	9
Saint Jerome's University	3	1.5	0	2	6.5
Saint John's University	4	3	5	2	14
Saint John's University	3	2	4	4	13
Saint Joseph's College of Maine	3	3	3	3	12
Saint Joseph's University	2	2.5	5	2	11.5
Saint Leo University	4	3	4	3	14
Saint Louis University	3	2	2	1	8
Saint Martin's University	3	1.5	1	2	7.5
Saint Mary-of-the-Woods College	3	1	1	2	7
Saint Mary's College (IN)	2	2.5	4	3	11.5
Saint Mary's College of California	3	2	3	2	10
Saint Mary's University (Canada)	2	1.5	1	1	5.5
Saint Mary's University (MN)	3	3	6	2	14
Saint Mary's University (TX)	3	3	3	3	12
Saint Michael's College	3	1.5	3	2	9.5
Saint Norbert College	4	3	4	2	13
Saint Olaf College	1	2.5	2	0	5.5
Saint Peter's University	3	2.5	3	3	11.5
Saint Paul University	2	2	2	1	7
Saint Thomas Aquinas College	3	1	1	2	7
Saint Thomas University (FL)	4	2.5	3	4	13.5

NAME	RHETORIC	MEMBERSHIP	CURRICULAR	CO-CURRIC	TOTAL
Saint Thomas University (Canada)	2	1.5	0	2	5.5
Saint Vincent College	3	2.5	5	3	13.5
Saint Xavier University	4	2.5	0	1	7.5
Salve Regina University	3	2.5	4	1	10.5
Samford University	4	3	3	5	15
San Diego Christian College	4	5	5	5	19
Santa Clara University	3	3	5	3	14
Schreiner University	1	0.5	0	1	2.5
Seattle Pacific University	4	5	5	4	18
Seattle University	1	1.5	3	3	8.5
Seton Hall University	3	3	4	1	11
Seton Hill University	4	2.5	2	2	10.5
Sewanee: University of the South	2	0.5	0	1	3.5
Shaw University	0	0	0	2	2
Shenandoah University	0	1.5	0	1	2.5
Shorter University (GA)	2	4	4	4	14
Siena College	3	2	2	3	10
Siena Heights University	4	2	0	1	7
Simmons College of Kentucky	4	5	10	3	22
Simpson College (IA)	0	0.5	0	1	1.5
Simpson University (CA)	3	5	5	5	18
Southeastern University	4	6	8	5	23
Southern Adventist University	4	5	4	5	18
Southern Nazarene University	4	4	3	5	16
Southern Wesleyan University	4	4	3	5	16
Southwest Baptist University	4	4	4	5	17
Southwestern Adventist University	3	5	5	3	16
Southwestern Assemblies of God U	3	5	5	5	18
Southwestern Christian University	4	5	5	5	19
Southwestern University	1	0	0	0	1

NAME	RHETORIC	MEMBERSHIP	CURRICULAR	CO-CURRIC	TOTAL
Spalding University	1	1.5	0	1	3.5
Spelman College	0	0	0	2	2
Spring Arbor University	4	5	4	5	18
Spring Hill College	4	1.5	1	4	10.5
Spurgeon College	4	5	11	5	25
Sterling College	4	5	4	4	17
Stillman College	1	0	5	5	11
Stonehill College	4	3	2	3	12
Summit Christian College	4	5	3	5	17
Tabor College	4	5	4	5	18
Taylor University	4	6	7	5	22
Tennessee Wesleyan University	1	1	0	3	5
Texas College	1	0	1	2	4
Texas Lutheran College	2	1.5	1	2	6.5
Texas Wesleyan University	1	0	0	0	1
The Catholic University of America	3	3	4	4	14
The King's University	4	5	4	3	16
The Master's University	4	6	8	5	23
The University of Findlay	2	0	0	1	3
Thiel College	1	1.5	0	1	3.5
Thomas Aquinas College	3	4	9	3	19
Thomas More College of Liberal Arts	4	3.5	8	3	18.5
Thomas More University	4	3.5	4	4	15.5
Toccoa Falls College	4	5	6	5	20
Tougaloo College	1	0	0	0	1
Trevecca Nazarene University	4	4	6	5	19
Trinity Baptist College	4	6	5	5	20
Trinity Christian College	4	4	5	4	17
Trinity International University	4	4	5	5	18
Trinity University	2	2.5	2	2	8.5

NAME	RHETORIC	MEMBERSHIP	CURRICULAR	CO-CURRIC	TOTAL
Trinity Western University	4	4	6	5	19
Truett McConnell University	4	5	6	4	19
Tusculum University	2	1.5	1	2	6.5
Tyndale University	4	5	6	3	18
Union College	2	5	4	3	14
Union University	4	5	3	5	17
University of Dallas	4	2	4	2	12
University of Dayton	4	3	3	3	13
University of Detroit Mercy	4	2	0	4	10
University of Dubuque	3	2	2	4	11
University of Fort Lauderdale	4	4	0	5	13
University of Holy Cross	3	3	2	1	9
University of Indianapolis	2	1.5	1	1	5.5
University of Jamestown	4	0	0	4	8
University of Lynchburg	1	0	0	0	1
University of Mary	3	1.5	4	4	12.5
University of Mary Hardin-Baylor	4	4	3	5	16
University of Mobile	4	4	3	5	16
University of Mount Olive	3	1	0	4	8
University of Northwestern-St. Paul	4	5	8	5	22
University of Notre Dame	4	3.5	5	3	15.5
University of Pikeville	3	0	1	1	5
University of Portland	3	2	4	4	13
University of Providence	4	2	3	4	13
University of Saint Francis (IL)	2	3	3	3	11
University of Saint Francis (IN)	3	2.5	2	2	9.5
University of Saint Joseph	2	1.5	4	1	8.5
University of Saint Mary (KS)	1	2	1	4	8
University of Saint Thomas (MN)	3	3	3	2	11
University of Saint Thomas (TX)	3	2	5	2	12

NAME	RHETORIC	MEMBERSHIP	CURRICULAR	CO-CURRIC	TOTAL
University of San Diego	3	2	3	1	9
University of San Francisco	3	2	2	2	9
University of Scranton	4	3	4	2	13
University of Sioux Falls	3	4	3	4	14
University of the Cumberlands	2	4	2	3	11
University of the Incarnate Word	4	2.5	1	2	9.5
University of the Ozarks	3	1	0	1	5
University of the Southwest	3	4	3	3	13
University of Tulsa	0	0	0	2	2
University of Valley Forge	4	5	6	5	20
Ursuline College	3	1.5	0	2	6.5
Valparaiso University	1	1.5	3	3	8.5
Vanguard University	3	5	7	5	20
Villa Maria College of Buffalo	3	3.5	1	2	9.5
Villanova University	4	3	5	3	15
Virginia Union University	0	0.5	2	2	4.5
Virginia University of Lynchburg	4	0	0	0	4
Virginia Wesleyan University	0	0.5	0	2	2.5
Viterbo University	3	2.5	2	3	10.5
Voorhees College	4	0	1	4	9
Waldorf University	2	0	1	2	5
Walla Walla University	4	5	5	4	18
Walsh University	4	2	2	2	10
Warner Pacific University	4	4	4	5	17
Warner University	4	4	3	5	16
Wartburg College	2	0.5	1	2	5.5
Washington Adventist University	2	2	1	5	10
Wayland Baptist University	4	4	3	5	16
Waynesburg University	4	4	2	2	12
Welch College	4	4	11	3	22

NAME	RHETORIC	MEMBERSHIP	CURRICULAR	CO-CURRIC	TOTAL
Wesleyan College (GA)	1	0	0	1	2
West Virginia Wesleyan College	2	0.5	1	1	4.5
Westminster College (PA)	2	1	1	2	6
Westmont College	4	4	5	5	18
Wheaton College (IL)	4	5	8	5	22
Wheeling University	3	2	2	3	10
Whitworth University	4	5	7	4	20
Wilberforce University	0	0	0	2	2
Wiley College	3	0	0	0	3
William Carey University	2	1.5	3	5	11.5
William Jessup University	4	4	8	5	21
William Penn University	1	0.5	2	3	6.5
William Woods University	1	0	0	2	3
Williams Baptist University	4	4	3	4	15
Wilmington College	2	1.5	1	3	7.5
Wilson College	0	0	0	2	2
Wingate University	2	0	1	1	4
Wisconsin Lutheran College	3	4	5	4	16
Wittenberg University	2	0.5	0	1	3.5
World Mission University	4	5	11	5	25
Wyoming Catholic College	3	4.5	8	5	20.5
Xavier University	3	2	6	2	13
Xavier University of Louisiana	3	1.5	4	3	11.5
York University	4	4	5	5	18

Notes

Introduction

1 Perry L. Glanzer, "BU's Stagnant Christian Commitment," *Waco Tribune-Herald*, December 5, 2021, 9; Perry L. Glanzer, "BU Must Pursue Christ-Animated Solutions," *Waco Tribune-Herald*, January 2, 2022, 9.

2 George M. Marsden, *The Soul of the American University: From Protestant Establishment to Established Nonbelief* (New York: Oxford University Press, 1994).

3 Perry L. Glanzer and Claudiu Cimpean, "The First Baptist University in Europe: An Explanation and Case Study," *Christian Higher Education* 8, no. 5 (2009): 1–11.

4 Donald G. Tewksbury, *The Founding of American Colleges and Universities before the Civil War* (New York: Teacher College Press, 1932), 32–54.

5 C. John Sommerville, "Secular Society / Religious Population: Our Tacit Rules for Using the Term 'Secularization,'" *Journal for the Scientific Study of Religion* 37, no. 2 (1998): 249–53.

6 George M. Marsden, *The Soul of the American University Revisited: From Protestant to Postsecular*, 2nd ed. (New York: Oxford University Press, 2021).

Chapter 1: What Makes a University Christian?

1 Perry L. Glanzer et al., "Are Nondenominational Colleges More Liberal Than Denominational Colleges? A Comparison of Faculty Beliefs," *Christian Higher Education* 18, no. 3 (2019): 207–23.

2 Robert Wood Lynn, "The Survival of Recognizably Protestant Colleges: Reflections on Old-Line Protestantism, 1950–1990," in *The Secularization of*

the Academy, ed. George M. Marsden and J. Bradley Longfield (New York: Oxford University Press, 1992), 180.

3 George M. Marsden, *The Soul of the American University Revisited: From Protestant to Postsecular*, 2nd ed. (New York: Oxford University Press, 2021).

4 Merrimon Cuninggim, *Uneasy Partners: The College and the Church* (Nashville: Abingdon, 1994), 3.

5 Richard G. Hutcheson, "Are Church-Related Colleges Also Christian Colleges?," *Christian Century* 105, no. 27 (1988): 840.

6 Cuninggim, *Uneasy Partners*, 98.

7 See Glanzer et al., "Are Nondenominational Colleges More Liberal?"

8 "Best Christian Colleges," EdSmart, https://www.edsmart.org/best-christian-colleges/.

9 "Mission & History," Texas Christian University, https://www.tcu.edu/about/mission-history.php.

10 "Mission, Vision, and Values," Biola University, https://www.biola.edu/about/mission.

11 "Colleges and Universities with Religious Affiliations," Encyclopedia.com, https://www.encyclopedia.com/education/encyclopedias-almanacs-transcripts-and-maps/colleges-and-universities-religious-affiliations.

12 "Fall Enrollment and Number of Degree-Granting Postsecondary Institutions, by Control and Religious Affiliation of Institution: Selected Years, 1980 through 2019," *Digest of Education Statistics*, National Center for Education Statistics, https://nces.ed.gov/programs/digest/d20/tables/dt20_303.90.asp.

Chapter 2: Mainline Protestant Colleges and Universities

1 According to our Google Ngram search, the term was used once in 1873 but then started to be used a bit more frequently in academic journals starting in the 1930s.

2 Perry L. Glanzer, *The Dismantling of Moral Education: How Higher Education Reduced the Human Identity* (Lanham, MD: Rowman & Littlefield, 2022).

3 For example, the United Methodist Higher Education Foundation still includes all the secularized schools on its list of Methodist institutions. "List

of United Methodist Schools," United Methodist Higher Education Foundation, https://www.umhef.org/about/schools/listofschools/.

4 Robert Benne, *Quality with Soul: How Six Premier Colleges and Universities Keep Faith with Their Religious Traditions* (Grand Rapids, MI: Eerdmans, 2001).

Chapter 3: Historically Black Colleges and Universities (HBCUs)

1 Henry Drewry and Humphrey Doermann, *Stand and Prosper: Private Black Colleges and Their Students* (Princeton, NJ: Princeton University Press, 2001), 37.

2 *Fisk University: History, Building and Site, and Services of Dedication* (New York: Trustees of Fisk University, 1876), 3.

3 James D. Anderson, *The Education of Blacks in the South, 1860–1935* (Chapel Hill: University of North Carolina Press, 1988), back cover.

4 Cynthia L. Jackson and Eleanor F. Nunn, *Historically Black Colleges and Universities: A Reference Handbook* (Santa Barbara, CA: ABC-CLIO, 2003), 51.

5 Drewry and Doermann, *Stand and Prosper*; Jackson and Nunn, *Historically Black Colleges and Universities*.

6 Joe E. Richardson, *A History of Fisk University, 1865–1946* (Birmingham: University of Alabama Press, 1980), 63.

7 *Spelman College Student Handbook and Resource Guide* (Atlanta: Spelman College, 2021), https://www.spelman.edu/docs/students/student-handbook.pdf.

8 Drewry and Doermann, *Stand and Prosper*, 61.

9 Juan Williams and Dwayne Ashley with Shawn Rhea, *I'll Find a Way or Make One: A Tribute to Historically Black Colleges and Universities* (San Francisco: Amistad/HarperCollins, 2004), 56–68.

10 Richardson, *History of Fisk University*, 85.

11 Drewry and Doermann, *Stand and Prosper*, 87.

12 Drewry and Doermann, 87.

13 Drewry and Doermann, 137.

14 Drewry and Doermann, 137.

15 Drewry and Doermann, 87.

16 Drewry and Doermann, 153.

17 See George M. Marsden, *The Soul of the American University: From Protestant Establishment to Established Nonbelief* (New York: Oxford University Press, 1994); and James T. Burtchaell, *The Dying of the Light: The Disengagement of Colleges and Universities from Their Christian Churches* (Grand Rapids, MI: Eerdmans, 1998).

18 Cassandra Chaney, "Religiosity and Spirituality among Members of an African American Church Community: A Qualitative Analysis," *Journal of Religion & Spirituality in Social Work* 27, no. 3 (2008): 201.

19 "Fall Enrollment, Degrees Conferred, and Expenditures in Degree-Granting Historically Black Colleges and Universities, by Institution: 2019, 2020, and 2019–20," *Digest of Education Statistics*, National Center for Education Statistics, https://nces.ed.gov/programs/digest/d21/tables/dt21_313.10.asp.

20 Octavio Ramirez et al., "Integration of Faith and Learning at a Faith-Based Historically Black University: An Exploratory Study," *Journal of Research on Christian Education* 29, no. 2 (2020): 127.

21 Benjamin B. Rawley, *History of Morehouse College* (Atlanta: Morehouse College, 1917), 81, https://dlg.usg.edu/record/dlg_zlgb_gb0312/fulltext.text.

22 "Sisters' Chapel," Spelman College, 2017, para. 2, https://www.spelman.edu/student-life/religious-life/sisters-chapel.

23 "Sisters' Chapel," para. 2.

24 Ramirez et al., "Integration of Faith and Learning," 126–36.

25 Ramirez et al., 131.

26 Ramirez et al., 131.

27 Ramirez et al., 132.

28 Perry L. Glanzer and Nathan F. Alleman, *The Outrageous Idea of Christian Teaching* (New York: Oxford University Press, 2019).

29 Joel C. Carpenter, Perry L. Glanzer, and Nicholas S. Lantinga, eds., *Christian Higher Education: A Global Reconnaissance* (Grand Rapids, MI: Eerdmans, 2014).

Chapter 4: Catholic Colleges and Universities

1 William P. Leahy, *Adapting to America Catholics: Jesuits, and Higher Education in the Twentieth Century* (Washington, DC: Georgetown University Press, 1991), 4; "Historical Summary of Faculty, Enrollment, Degrees Conferred, and Finances in Degree-Granting Postsecondary Institutions: Selected Years, 1869–70 through 2018–19," *Digest of Education Statistics*, National Center for Education Statistics, https://nces.ed.gov/programs/digest/d20/tables/dt20_301.20.asp?current=yes.

2 Philip Gleason, *Contending with Modernity: Catholic Higher Education in the Twentieth Century* (New York: Oxford University Press, 1995); R. Hassenger, *The Shape of Catholic Higher Education* (Chicago: University of Chicago Press, 1967); Tracy Schier and Cynthia Russett, *Catholic Women's Colleges in America* (Baltimore: Johns Hopkins University Press, 2002).

3 Philip Gleason, "American Catholic Higher Education, 1940–1990: The Ideological Context," in *The Secularization of the Academy*, ed. George C. Marsden and Bradley J. Longfield (New York: Oxford University Press, 1992), 180–87, 234; "Historical Summary of Faculty."

4 John Paul II, "Apostolic Constitution of the Supreme Pontiff John Paul II on Catholic Universities," Vatican, https://www.vatican.va/content/john-paul -ii/en/apost_constitutions/documents/hf_jp-ii_apc_15081990_ex-corde -ecclesiae.html.

5 Paul D. Sullins, "The Difference Catholic Makes: Catholic Faculty and Catholic Identity," *Journal for the Scientific Study of Religion* 43, no. 1 (2004): 83–101; Sandra M. Estanek, Michael James, and Daniel Norton, "Assessing Catholic Identity: A Study of Mission Statements of Catholic Colleges and Universities," *Catholic Education (Dayton, Ohio)* 10, no. 2 (2006): 199–217; Robert Abelman and Amy Dalessandro, "An Assessment of the Institutional Vision of Catholic Colleges and Universities," *Catholic Education (Dayton, Ohio)* 12, no. 2 (2008): 221–35; Stephen F. Gambescia and Rocco Paolucci, "Nature and Extent of Catholic Identity Communicated through Official Websites of U.S. Catholic Colleges and Universities," *Catholic Education (Dayton, Ohio)* 15, no. 1 (2011): 3– 27; Roger Pizarro Milian and Jessica Rizk, "Marketing Catholic

Higher Education: Holistic Self-Actualization, Personalized Learning, and Wholesome Goodness," *Higher Education* 76, no. 1 (2018): 51–66.

6 James L. Heft, *The Future of Catholic Higher Education* (New York: Oxford University Press, 2021).

Chapter 5: Evangelical Colleges and Universities in Multidenominational Coalitions

1 See Thomas S. Kidd, *Who Is an Evangelical? The History of a Movement in Crisis* (New Haven, CT: Yale University Press, 2019).

2 James A. Patterson, *Shining Lights: A History of the Council for Christian Colleges & Universities* (Grand Rapids, MI: Baker Academic, 2001).

3 "Our Institutions: Overview," CCCU.org, https://www.cccu.org/institutions/#heading-categories-3.

4 The employment policies of CCCU state, "CCCU governing and associate members have a continuing institutional policy and practice, effective throughout membership, to hire as full-time faculty members and administrators only persons who profess faith in Jesus Christ." See "Our Institutions."

5 Sarah Eekhoff Zylstra, "Crisis Averted," *Christianity Today*, November 2015, 24.

6 "Membership Overview," IACE, https://iace.education/membership-overview.

7 "Membership Directory," IACE, https://iace.education/membership-directory.

Chapter 6: Independent Low Church Protestant Colleges and Universities

1 Pepperdine, Abilene Christian, and Lipscomb University have sought membership in the CCCU and are treated in the previous chapter. The other institutions broadly affiliated with Churches of Christ are covered in this chapter.

Chapter 7: The One Eastern Orthodox College

1 Rashdall Hastings, *The Universities of Europe in the Middle Ages*, ed. Frederick Maurice Powicke and Alfred Brotherston Emden (New York: Oxford

University Press, 1997); Willem Frijhoff, "Patterns," in *A History of the University in Europe*, ed. Hilde de Ridder-Symoens, vol. 2, *Universities in Early Modern Europe* (New York: Cambridge University Press, 1996), 43–110.

2 In *Eastern Orthodox Christianity and American Higher Education*, Elizabeth H. Prodromou tries to downplay this claim, but we do not find her argument convincing, as the role of the Russian patriarch in the recent war with Ukraine evidences. See Ann Mitsakos Bezzerides and Elizabeth H. Prodromou, eds., *Eastern Orthodox Christianity and American Higher Education: Theological, Historical, and Contemporary Reflections* (Notre Dame, IN: University of Notre Dame Press, 2017).

3 Timothy Ware, *The Orthodox Church*, rev. ed. (New York: Penguin, 1997); Steven Runciman, *The Great Church in Captivity: A Study of the Patriarchate of Constantinople from the Eve of the Turkish Conquest to the Greek War of Independence* (New York: Cambridge University Press, 1968).

4 Alexander Schmemann, *The Historical Road of Eastern Orthodoxy*, trans. Lydia W. Kesich (New York: Holt, Rinehart & Winston, 1963), 281–84.

5 See Alexei Nesteruk, *Light from the East: Theology, Science and the Eastern Orthodox Tradition* (Minneapolis: Fortress, 2003), 51.

6 Daniel Clendenin, *Eastern Orthodox Christianity: A Western Perspective* (Grand Rapids, MI: Baker Books, 2003), 53–54.

7 Nesteruk, *Light from the East*, 38.

8 Some scholars try to claim the Capitol School established in Constantinople in the sixth century and the Kievan Academy of the Middle Ages as universities. See, for example, James Brown, *A History of Western Education* (New York: St. Martin's Press, 1972), 1:294. In *A History of Christian Education: Protestant, Catholic and Orthodox Perspectives* (Malabar, FL: Krieger, 2002), John Elias, clearly borrowing from Brown, calls the Capital School "the first institution of higher Christian studies in Christendom" (232). J. M. Hussey in *Church and Learning in the Byzantine Empire, 867–1185* (New York: Russell & Russell, 1963) calls the Capital School a university. The vast majority of contemporary higher education historians, however, would reject these claims. See, for example, N. G. Wilson, *Scholars of Byzantium* (Baltimore: Johns Hopkins University Press, 1983), 49–50. In fact, in an essay on the history of universities, Jacques Verger writes, "No one today would dispute

the fact that universities, in the sense in which the term is now generally understood, were a creation of the Middle Ages, appearing for the first time between the twelfth and thirteenth centuries." See Jacques Verger, "Patterns," in *A History of the University in Europe*, ed. Hilde de Ridder-Symoens, vol. 1, *Universities in the Middle Ages* (New York: Cambridge University Press, 1992), 35.

9 "A Brief History of Hellenic College Holy Cross," Hellenic College Holy Cross, https://www.hchc.edu/why-hchc/#mission-vision-values.

10 "Brief History of Hellenic College."

Chapter 8: Evaluating the Diversity of Christian Higher Education in the United States

1 George D. Kuh et al., *Student Success in College: Creating Conditions That Matter* (San Francisco: Jossey-Bass, 2010), 26.

2 Kuh et al., 26.

3 For literature on the particularities of Christian higher education, see Robert Benne, *Quality with Soul: How Six Premier Colleges and Universities Keep Faith with Their Religious Traditions* (Grand Rapids, MI: Eerdmans, 2001); Richard T. Hughes and William B. Adrian, eds., *Models for Christian Higher Education: Strategies for Survival and Success in the Twenty-First Century* (Grand Rapids, MI: Eerdmans, 1997); and William C. Ringenberg, *The Christian College: A History of Protestant Higher Education in America*, 2nd ed. (Grand Rapids, MI: Baker Academic, 2012).

4 Carnegie classifies the breadth of Christian institutions under the "faith-based" category. See "Basic Classification Description," in *The Carnegie Classification of Institutions of Higher Education* (Washington, DC: American Council on Education, 2022), https://carnegieclassifications.acenet.edu/classification_descriptions/basic.php. Additionally, the well-known anthology of the effects of college does not provide any institutional granularity beyond "Christian institutions" or "Christian colleges and universities." See Matthew J. Mayhew et al., *How College Affects Students: 21st Century Evidence That Higher Education Works*, vol. 3 (San Francisco: John Wiley & Sons, 2016).

5 John Barnard, *From Evangelicalism to Progressivism at Oberlin College, 1966–1917* (Columbus: Ohio State University Press, 1969).

6 Andrea L. Turpin, *A New Moral Vision: Gender, Religion, and the Changing Purposes of American Higher Education, 1837–1917* (Ithaca, NY: Cornell University Press, 2016).

7 David W. Bebbington, *Evangelicalism in Modern Britain: A History from the 1730s to the 1980s* (London: Unwin Hyman, 1989).

8 See James T. Burtchaell, *The Dying of the Light: The Disengagement of Colleges and Universities from Their Christian Churches* (Grand Rapids, MI: Eerdmans, 1998); and Perry L. Glanzer et al., "Are Nondenominational Colleges More Liberal Than Denominational Colleges? A Comparison of Faculty Beliefs," *Christian Higher Education* 18, no. 3 (2019): 207–23.

Chapter 9: A New Vision for US Christian Higher Education

1 Ellen Bara Stolzenberg et al., "The American Freshman: National Norms Fall 2019," in *Cooperative Institutional Research Program* (Los Angeles: Higher Education Research Institute, UCLA, 2020).

2 George M. Marsden, *The Soul of the American University: From Protestant Establishment to Established Nonbelief* (New York: Oxford University Press, 1994); Charles E. Cotherman, *To Think Christianly: A History of L'abri, Regent College, and the Christian Study Center Movement* (Downers Grove, IL: InterVarsity, 2020).

3 The literature on CCT that does exist includes the following: Cotherman, *To Think Christianly*; Andrew Hansen, "A Christian College in a Food Truck? Christian Study Centers and Moral Formation," *International Journal of Christianity & Education* 25, no. 1 (March 2021): 83–95, https://doi.org/10.1177/2056997120971656; and David C. Mahan and C. Donald Smedley, "University Ministry and the Evangelical Mind," in *The State of the Evangelical Mind: Reflections on the Past, Prospects for the Future*, ed. Todd C. Ream, Jerry Pattengale, and Christopher J. Devers (Downers Grove, IL: InterVarsity, 2018), 59–99.

4 Hansen, "Christian College in a Food Truck?," 88.

5 Cotherman, *To Think Christianly*.

6 "Who We Are," Consortium of Christian Study Centers, 2020, https://cscmovement.org/who-we-are/#StudyCenter.

7 The term *faithful presence* was referenced by many center leaders we interviewed, several of whom hinted that they were borrowing the term from James Davison Hunter, *To Change the World: The Irony, Tragedy, and Possibility of Christianity in the Late Modern World* (New York: Oxford University Press, 2010).

8 Cotherman, *To Think Christianly.*

9 The language of "thick moral communities" comes from James Davison Hunter, *The Death of Character: Moral Education in an Age without Good or Evil* (New York: Basic Books, 2000).

10 "About: What Is Christian Higher Education?," CCCU.org, 2022, https://www.cccu.org/about/#heading-what-is-christian-higher-3.

11 See, for example, George M. Marsden, *The Outrageous Idea of Christian Scholarship* (New York: Oxford University Press, 1997); Mark A. Noll, *Jesus Christ and the Life of the Mind* (Grand Rapids, MI: Eerdmans, 2011); David Smith, *On Christian Teaching: Practicing Faith in the Classroom* (Grand Rapids, MI: Eerdmans, 2018); Perry L. Glanzer and Nathan F. Alleman, *The Outrageous Idea of Christian Teaching* (Oxford: Oxford University Press, 2019); and Oliver D. Crisp et al., eds., *Christianity and the Disciplines* (London: T&T Clark, 2014).

12 Perry L. Glanzer, "Christian Scholarly Creativity: A New Year's Assessment and Call," *Faith Animating Learning* (blog), January 4, 2021, https://christianscholars.com/christian-scholarly-creativity-a-new-years-assessment-and-call/.

13 Theodore F. Cockle, Perry L. Glanzer, and Madeline Whitmore, "Faculty Development for Christian Mission: The State of the Field," *Christian Higher Education* 21, no. 5 (2022): 337–401, https://doi.org/10.1080/15363759.2022.2029622.

14 See Hansen, "Christian College in a Food Truck?"

15 Perry L. Glanzer et al., *Christ-Enlivened Student Affairs: A Guide to Christian Thinking and Practice in the Field* (Abilene, TX: ACU Press, 2020).

16 Robert Birnbaum, *How Colleges Work: The Cybernetics of Academic Organization and Leadership*, 1st ed., Jossey-Bass Higher Education Series (San Francisco: Jossey-Bass, 1988).

17 Theodore F. Cockle, Sinda K. Vanderpool, and David Q. Hao, "Thinking Theologically about Student Success: Higher Education with a Higher Calling," *International Journal of Christianity & Education*, October 26, 2022, 1–24, https://doi.org/10.1177/20569971221130009; Perry L. Glanzer, Nathan F. Alleman, and Todd C. Ream, *Restoring the Soul of the University: Unifying Christian Higher Education in a Fragmented Age* (Downers Grove, IL: InterVarsity, 2017).

18 Glanzer, Alleman, and Ream, *Restoring the Soul of the University*, 231.

19 Alasdair C. MacIntyre, *After Virtue: A Study in Moral Theory*, 3rd ed. (Notre Dame, IN: University of Notre Dame Press, 2007), 33.

Chapter 10: Canadian Christian Colleges and Universities

1 Louis Cornelissen, "Religiosity in Canada and Its Evolution from 1985 to 2019," Statistics Canada, October 28, 2021, https://www150.statcan.gc.ca/n1/pub/75-006-x/2021001/article/00010-eng.htm; Jeffrey M. Jones, "How Religious Are Americans?," Gallup, December 23, 2021, https://news.gallup.com/poll/358364/religious-americans.aspx.

2 "Total Fall Enrollment in Degree-Granting Postsecondary Institutions, by Attendance Status, Sex of Student, and Control of Institution: Selected Years, 1947 through 2030," *Digest of Education Statistics*, National Center for Education Statistics, https://nces.ed.gov/programs/digest/d21/tables/dt21_303.10.asp?current=yes.

3 Robin S. Harris, *A History of Higher Education in Canada, 1663–1960* (Toronto: University of Toronto Press, 1976).

4 See Catherine Gidney, *A Long Eclipse: The Liberal Protestant Establishment and the Canadian University, 1920–1970* (Montreal: McGill-Queen's University Press, 2004); and Terence J. Fay, *A History of Canadian Catholics: Gallicanism, Romanism, and Canadianism* (Montreal: McGill-Queen's University Press, 2002).

5 Harry Fernhout, "Quest for Identity and Place: Christian University Education in Canada," in *Christian Higher Education: A Global Reconnaissance*, ed. Joel C. Carpenter, Perry L. Glanzer, and Nicholas S. Lantinga (Grand Rapids, MI: Eerdmans, 2014), 231.

Conclusion: Using the Results of Our Guide

1 Perry L. Glanzer et al., *Christ-Enlivened Student Affairs: A Guide to Christian Thinking and Practice in the Field* (Abilene, TX: ACU Press, 2020), 134–35.

2 Glanzer et al.

3 There is a tool on the *Chronicle of Higher Education* website for examining who institutions list as their peer institutions. See Jacquelyn Elias, "Who Does Your College Think Its Peers Are," *Chronicle of Higher Education*, March 24, 2022, https://www.chronicle.com/article/who-does-your-college-think-its-peers-are/. It is based on whether an institution views all/most, about half, a minority, or none of its peers as other faith-based institutions.

4 Reinhold Niebuhr, *Moral Man and Immoral Society: A Study in Ethics and Politics* (Louisville, KY: Westminster John Knox Press, 2001).

5 This outlook also results in tragic blind spots. To use our institution as an example, see Tawnell D. Hobbs and Andrea Fuller, "How Baylor Steered Lower-Income Parents to Debt They Couldn't Afford," *Wall Street Journal*, October 13, 2021. The article chronicles how "parents at Baylor University had the worst repayment rate for a type of federal loan called Parent Plus among private schools with at least a $1 billion endowment" and notes, "Among wealthy colleges, though, Baylor is one of the least generous with aid to needy students, publicly available documents show." This approach is not Christ-animated administration.

6 "R1" is shorthand for "Research 1" status, the highest ranking awarded by the Carnegie Classification of Institutions of Higher Education to universities that meet benchmarks in research activity and expenditures. The designation "Doctoral / Very High Research Activity" is also sometimes used to categorize these institutions.

7 See, for example, "Baylor Regents Hear Progress Report on University's R1 Goals, Illuminate Strategic Plan," Baylor University, July 16, 2021, https://www.baylor.edu/mediacommunications/news.php?action=story&story=224080.

8 "Baylor among Elite Group of Private R1 Institutions," Baylor University, December 19, 2021, https://www.baylor.edu/research/news.php?action=story&story=225970.

9 Kevin Dougherty et al., "Baylor Faith and Character Study: Methods and Preliminary Findings," *Christian Higher Education* 21, no. 3 (2021): 168–90, https://doi.org/10.1080/15363759.2021.1929564. For additional reflection on how to think theologically about student success, see Theodore F. Cockle, Sinda K. Vanderpool, and David Q. Hao, "Thinking Theologically about Student Success: Higher Education with a Higher Calling," *International Journal of Christianity & Education*, 2022, 1–24, https://doi.org/10.1177/20569971221130009.

10 Glanzer et al., *Christ-Enlivened Student Affairs*, 39.

11 Todd C. Ream and Perry L. Glanzer, *The Idea of a Christian College: A Reexamination for Today's University* (Eugene, OR: Cascade Books, 2013), 53.

12 Britney N. Graber, "Incompatible? How Christian Faith Informs Title IX Policy and Practice" (PhD diss., Baylor University, 2021).

13 Paul's encouragement to "put off" and "put on" in Ephesians comes to mind here. It is not enough to "put off your old self" (Eph. 4:22); we must also "put on the new self" (Eph. 4:24). The Christian life is about not merely avoiding certain behaviors but a positive reordering of our loves to worship rightly.

14 Associate Deans (@ass_deans), "It is that time of year when the college wants to thank all our faculty and staff for their hard work this year. Not with money, support, or resources," Twitter, November 14, 2021, 8:28 a.m., https://twitter.com/ass_deans/status/1459890995261321220.

15 Theodore F. Cockle, Perry L. Glanzer, and Madeline Whitmore, "Faculty Development for Christian Mission: The State of the Field," *Christian Higher Education* 21, no. 5 (2022): 337–401, https://doi.org/10.1080/15363759.2022.2029622.

16 See Kristen A. Renn and Jennifer Hodges, "The First Year on the Job: Experiences of New Professionals in Student Affairs," *Journal of Student Affairs Research and Practice* 44, no. 2 (2007): 604–28.

THE HISPANIC FACULTY EXPERIENCE

Opportunities for Growth and Retention in Christian Colleges and Universities

EDITED BY
OCTAVIO J. ESQUEDA AND BENJAMIN D. ESPINOZA

ISBN 978-1-68426-229-8

Hispanics are not a current trend.

Every racial term—including Hispanic, Latino/a, and more recently Latinx and Latine—is imperfect and problematic. There is no consensus about what works best. Despite this reality, the lives and stories of non-White faculty are essential to the future of Christian higher education.

Filled with triumphs, struggles, and penetrating insights, *The Hispanic Faculty Experience* explains what it is like to experience the shifting demographics of today's universities, which are bringing increasing numbers of Hispanic students even as the overall number of Hispanic colleagues remains exceedingly small.

This book will be especially useful for leaders who may be unaware of how difficult it is to navigate the challenges of Christian higher education as Hispanic faculty.

"This anthology brings a seasoned, informed, and thoughtful group of Latina/o scholars and educators to share eloquently about their joys and pains, their struggles and achievements, and their sacrifices and victories in following a personal and Christian vocation in predominantly White schools within the orbit of Christian Colleges and Universities."

—**Luis R. Rivera-Rodríguez,** Vice President of the Hispanic Association for Theological Education

1-877-816-4455 toll free
acupressbooks.com

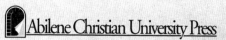
Abilene Christian University Press

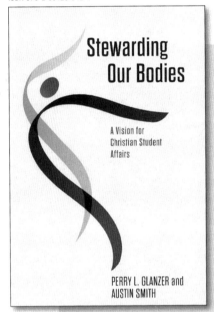
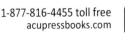

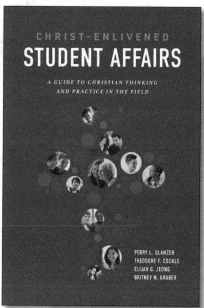

WHY COLLEGE MATTERS TO GOD

An Introduction to Christian Learning

RICK OSTRANDER

ISBN 978-1-68426-191-8

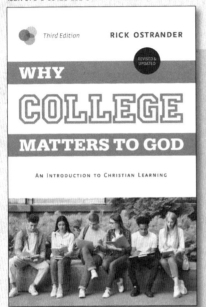

A trusted first-year text at Christian colleges and universities

Why College Matters to God is a brief, easy-to-read introduction to the unique purpose of a Christian college education. It has been widely used by Christian colleges and universities over the past decade because of its unsurpassed ability to be substantive yet accessible. The book draws on the insights of a wide range of Christian philosophers, theologians, historians, and scientists, but communicates key concepts in straightforward language that connects with a general audience. Brief enough to be paired with other texts, *Why College Matters to God* is an ideal introduction to the why and how of Christian learning for students, faculty, staff, and parents.

The third edition preserves the qualities of the previous editions along with updated illustrations and new material on important topics, such as . . .

- Christian learning and the challenges of technology
- Christian vocation, career preparation, and the liberal arts
- Diversity and civility on campus
- The habits of the highly effective college student

"The crisp, conversational quality of *Why College Matters to God* makes it remarkably accessible for college students. For all its ease of reading, the book also bears the marks of a wise grasp of the biblical and theological grounds for learning, the history of higher education, and our present cultural moment. Combining evident faith and generous understanding, Rick has given us a fabulous resource to make good Christian sense of a college education."

—**Douglas V. Henry,** Dean of the Honors College, Baylor University

1-877-816-4455 toll free
acupressbooks.com
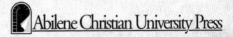